Hope in the Midst of the Storm

CAROL E. HORNER

Scriptures taken from the Holy Bible, New International Version®, NIV®. Copyright © 1973, 1978, 1984, 2011 by Biblica, Inc.™ Used by permission of Zondervan. All rights reserved worldwide. www.zondervan.com The "NIV" and "New International Version" are trademarks registered in the United States Patent and Trademark Office by Biblica, Inc.™

The author's royalties from this book will go toward sending mission teams from her church on summer work trips.

DEDICATION

This book is dedicated to Jesus, for healing
my heart and giving me hope for the future.
I'll love you, trust you, and follow you forever.

A man's heart plans his way,
But the Lord directs his steps.

~ Proverbs 16:9

CONTENTS

ACKNOWLEDGMENTS

I would like to thank ...

My pastor, Dan Oldham, who encouraged me to write this book. Your prayers and support got me through some tough times. Thanks for believing in me and always telling me to "just have faith."

My mom, Emily Deremer, who has always supported my many endeavors. Thanks for all the time you took to proofread and correct my many rough drafts.

My good friend, Barbara Allison, for her time and efforts in assisting in the proofreading and editing process.

My best friend, Lori Claar. You were always there for me. I could always count on you no matter what was going on in my life. I miss you greatly, but I know you are singing and dancing with the King of Glory!

My good friends, Kim Livingston, Tammy Kerr, and Amy Oldham, who loved and supported me through some tough times this past year. Thank you for all your hugs, emails, and texts.

My daughter, Beth, who blesses my life in ways she will never fully know or understand. Thanks for being my biggest cheerleader. I love you!

My husband, Randy. God has been so good to us! When we said for better or worse twenty-eight years ago, we had no idea what was about to come our way. I love you!

INTRODUCTION

Life is full of ups and downs, heartaches and joy. I've often said that I am on a journey and my ultimate destination is heaven. It hasn't been an easy journey, but God never promised that it would be. He did promise that no matter what I go through in this life, he will be there right beside me. That gives me great confidence and hope. This book is filled with real events from my life. In some cases, I've changed a few details to protect the privacy of others.

Some of these events have been so painful that I thought I would never recover. I've learned in those hard times not to pretend that everything is OK and under control when it's not. Until I was willing to acknowledge each of my situations for exactly what they were, I couldn't experience healing. Bad things happen to all of us. We have a choice in what we do about it. We can wrap our arms around the pain and live like a victim the rest of our life, or we can discover that God has a purpose for our pain. When we reach out to God, he takes our hand and walks us through it.

There are a variety of ways you can use this book. You can sit and read it straight through like a normal book. You can use it as a spring board to a group discussion, or you can even use it as a devotional. I encourage you to have your Bible and a pen handy. Make notes on things you want to revisit. Write down what God is teaching you through each lesson. I have been so glad that I have been journaling through my journey, and that I had those writings to go back and read. As I reread those journals, I saw the grace of God, the strength of God, and the love of God on each page. I saw how he walked beside me and grew me through each hurt.

God longs to meet us where we are. Our journeys through life are filled with many storms. Some are small like a spring shower and others have the force of a hurricane.

If you are in the middle of one of these storms, God is there. He can handle your tears, your fears, and your anger. He understands your feelings. Embrace him. Trust him. Allow him to heal your heart and show you that there is "Hope in the Midst of the Storm."

1 THE STORM OF HOPELESSNESS

Life today can be really tough. Just read the newspaper and you will see reports of crimes, natural disasters, unemployment, economic turmoil, and political chaos. It screams that the future is uncertain and that there is little hope. It is comforting to recognize that God knows and understands everything that is going on. He also knows what the future holds. He is not surprised by any of this.

I don't think our feelings of hopelessness are new. I think they have existed since Bible times. The story of Jonah is a good example. If anyone had a reason to feel hopeless, I think Jonah did. You remember the story. Jonah was disobedient to God and so God sent a great fish to swallow Jonah. As Jonah was riding around the ocean inside this fish, he knew he was there because of his own defiance. He knew he couldn't get himself out of that terrible situation. He realized that he had nowhere to turn but to God, and so all of Jonah chapter 2 is his prayer while he is in the fish. Jonah remembered who God is and had faith. In verse 9, Jonah says, "Salvation comes from the Lord."

I'm not sure I would have had the same attitude and prayer if I was inside the belly of a fish, sitting alongside of partially digested fish food, in the dark, covered with stomach juices, with seaweed wrapped around my head!

What happens next in the story? The Lord commanded the fish to vomit Jonah up onto dry land. God was not done with Jonah yet, he just needed to get his attention. Sitting in fish vomit would definitely have gotten my attention!

Hope today has a definition completely different from the biblical term *hope*. In the English language the word hope carries the idea of uncertainty. As in – I hope it won't rain today. I hope my football team will win. I hope my children do well in school. I hope I don't lose my job.

In the New Testament, the word hope carries the idea of certainty. If God says something is going to happen in the future, we can expect it without any doubt. This is real hope - the certainty that everything God has promised, he will fulfill. For a Christian, hope is also found in the promise that God will never leave us or forsake us (Deuteronomy 31:6).

I think God allows us to experience situations that seem hopeless so that we will look to him and see him more clearly. Remember the story of Elisha and his servant from 2 Kings 6. The king of Aram was at war with Israel, and he was angry because Elisha was able to predict where his army was planning to go. Elisha warned the King of Israel so he and his men could plan their strategy. The king of Aram sent a large deployment of soldiers out to capture Elisha, so he wouldn't be able to help Israel win the war. Elisha's servant got up one morning and saw that they were surrounded by a large army. He had no way of escape, and he was afraid. In verses 16-17, Elisha told his servant not to be afraid because "those who are with us are more than those who are with them." Then Elisha asked God to open the eyes of his servant so he could see. When he did, the servant saw the hills full of horses and chariots of fire all around Elisha. The servant was able to see the angelic army that God had sent there to protect them. God was showing these men that what appeared impossible for man was not impossible for God.

Sometimes we have to get to the end of our rope in order for God to open our eyes and let us see that he is still in control. Sometimes it takes being hopeless for us to call out to God and trust him the most.

Hopeless situations have a way of reminding us of our ultimate hope. They get our focus off this life. They have a way of stripping our lives down to the bare necessities - what is really important to us. It is so easy to put our hope in things of this world. It is easy to trust in our jobs, money, positions, and achievements. They are tangible assets. Sometimes it takes a crisis in our lives to get us to refocus on what is really important. It takes being confronted with some kind of hopelessness for us to see that all the things of this world are temporary. When our hope is in the wrong things, we are set up for disappointment. It is in those times that we get our focus back on God. One of the best ways to protect ourselves from despair and hopelessness is not to fall in love with the things of this world. We need to work on maintaining an eternal perspective.

Too many Christians act as if this life is all there is. Remember where our citizenship lies – in heaven. That's where our ultimate hope is.

Some hopeless situations in this life will not change. You may be asking questions like, why did I get this disease, why doesn't my spouse believe, why did I lose my job, why can't I have children, why can't I get married, why…, why…, why…? You are not the only person struggling with issues like these.

Jeremiah 15:18 asks a similar question, "Why is my pain unending and my wound grievous and incurable?" What Jeremiah was really asking is, "God, can I trust you?"

As I've experienced hard times in my life, I've asked the same question. Perhaps I didn't know that was the question I was asking, but when I question why things are happening to me, I am really asking - Can I trust God? Does he really love me? Is he really on my side? Will he take care of me? What I've seen is that God loves me and provides me with the strength I need to handle the circumstances that life has thrown at me. He used the hard times to force me to turn to him. When I prayed for God to change my situation, God answered that he wanted to change me. He was and is committed to finishing what he has started in my life. He is more concerned with my character than he is with my circumstances or my comfort. I experienced hope as I submitted myself to God and allowed him to work in my life through my circumstances.

Going back to the story of Jonah, he had nowhere to turn but to God. Oftentimes in our lives, we wait until we've exhausted all our other options and then we call on God. What we really need to do, is see God as our first choice. We need to trust him completely.

God was teaching Jonah this lesson because he wanted him to serve him with his whole heart. God had a specific plan for Jonah. Jonah needed to humble himself and acknowledge that God was in control. He needed to surrender his life and his plans to God. He needed to obey God and do what God asked him to do even if he didn't agree with it. Only as he did these things was God able to use him to reach the Ninevites.

So where are you today? Are you able to have hope when things seem hopeless? Do you see hopeless situations as allowed in your life by God? Do you believe that God can and will use it to develop your character? Are you able to see that the real battle belongs to the Lord?

For further thought:

"Therefore, since we have been justified through faith, we have peace with God through our Lord Jesus Christ, through whom we have gained access by faith into this grace in which we now stand. And we boast in the hope of the glory of God. Not only so, but we also glory in our sufferings, because we know that suffering produces perseverance; perseverance, character; and character, hope. And hope does not put us to shame, because God's love has been poured out into our hearts through the Holy Spirit, who has been given to us." (Romans 5:1-5)

"Blessed are those whose help is the God of Jacob, whose hope is in the Lord their God. He is the Maker of heaven and earth, the sea, and everything in them - he remains faithful forever. He upholds the cause of the oppressed and gives food to the hungry. The Lord sets prisoners free, the Lord gives sight to the blind, the Lord lifts up those who are bowed down, the Lord loves the righteous." (Psalm 146: 5-8)

"May the God of hope fill you with all joy and peace as you trust in him, so that you may overflow with hope by the power of the Holy Spirit." (Romans 15:13)

2 THE STORM OF WORRY

I've spent a lot of time in my life worrying about things. I've worried about my daughter, safety, money, work, grades, time, and bills. I've even worried about having my house clean before company arrived. I've worried about the dog. I'm an accomplished worrier. It comes naturally to me and really didn't take much practice. I don't even want to think about how many hours I've wasted in my lifetime by worrying. I've begun to realize something that I should have learned a long time ago, things just aren't worth worrying about.

Worrying is the opposite of trusting. It takes my focus off of things that are important. It causes me to focus on things that really aren't important or in some cases, things I can't do anything about anyway. It wastes my time and therefore, my life. Worrying never solves any of my problems; it just creates more. It can destroy my energy and my strength. Corrie Ten Boom once said that, "worry does not empty tomorrow of its sorrow; it empties today of its strength."[1]

I am a strong, independent woman, and sometimes I start to think that I can solve my own problems. I start relying on myself when I should be relying on God. 1 Peter 5:6-7 says, "Humble yourselves, therefore, under God's mighty hand, that he may lift you up in due time. Cast all your anxiety on him because he cares for you."

There are two important steps to this verse. The first one is that I am to humble myself. I need to quit trying to do things for myself. As long as I am depending on myself and not God, I will worry. The second part says I am to cast all my anxiety on him. I must trust him to take care of me, and I must rest in his care.

Sometimes we don't want to admit we are worried about something, so we say we are concerned. Does changing the word really change the situation? Sometimes we don't want to tell someone we are worried about something, and so we "share it" as a prayer request. Does that really change what is in our heart? We need to be honest with ourselves and identify the things or situations in our lives that cause us to worry.

Situations come up almost every day that cause me worry. It's what I do with that worry that matters. Do I give it to the Lord and take my hands off of it? Do I trust God to handle the situation, or do I try to help? Here's a hint - God doesn't need our help. When I pray about it and leave it in God's hands, I don't get to choose the answer that God gives me. I need to be willing to accept his solution.

I need to come to the place where pleasing God is the only thing that matters in my life. If I love the Lord with all my heart, the way I am commanded to, then pleasing him will be foremost on my mind. I can't trust God and worry at the same time.

So how do you get rid of worry in your life? I think a good starting point is focusing on the truth in the Bible. Open it and start reading. If you've never read the Bible before, the book of John is a good place to begin. Learn what God says through his Word. When you find a particular part that helps, meditate on it and get it into your mind and heart. When hard situations come along, these truths are the things that will guide your thoughts and actions.

The next step would be prayer. Jesus prayed about everything, and if he needed to pray, how much more do I need to pray. Paul writes in Philippians 4:6-7, "Do not be anxious about anything, but in every situation, by prayer and petition, with thanksgiving, present your requests to God. And the peace of God, which transcends all understanding, will guard your hearts and your minds in Christ Jesus."

As we give our requests to God and trust him to handle the situation, God's peace will fill our hearts. There won't be any room for worry. Paul goes on to tell us what we should focus our minds on in order to experience the peace of God.

> Whatever is true, whatever is noble, whatever is right, whatever is pure, whatever is lovely, whatever is admirable - if anything is excellent or praiseworthy - think about such things. Whatever you have learned or received or heard from me, or seen in me - put it into practice. And the God of peace will be with you. (Philippians 4:8-9)

We all make choices every day, and choosing what to think about is one of them. I can choose to worry, or I can choose to trust God. God doesn't force me to trust him; it is in choosing to trust him that I show him I love him.

So what's your choice going to be today - worry or trust? I choose trust.

For further thought:

"Trust in the LORD with all your heart and lean not on your own understanding; in all your ways acknowledge him, and he will make your paths straight." (Proverbs 3:5-6)

"Can any one of you by worrying add a single hour to your life?" (Matthew 6:27)

"But seek first his kingdom and his righteousness, and all these things will be given to you as well. Therefore do not worry about tomorrow, for tomorrow will worry about itself. Each day has enough trouble of its own." (Matthew 6:33-34)

3 THE STORM OF BROKENNESS

Brokenness is not something we really want to think about. It sounds painful. However, brokenness is necessary in the Christian life if we are going to grow and become all that God wants for us to be. Brokenness is God's way of dealing with our self-reliance. God uses different events and even trials in our lives to break our independent spirits. Brokenness is not weakness, and it's not punishment.

My husband and I plant a garden each year. As I am writing this, I am reminded about when we plant a seed in the ground. Seeds are typically hard. If we look carefully at a seed, it is difficult to believe that life can come from it. Only as we plant seeds can they go on to accomplish their purpose. In the soil they receive what they need to break the hard outer shell. It is only as the shell is broken that the plant can sprout, grow, and produce.[1]

Jesus taught about this principle in John 12 when he said, "unless a kernel of wheat falls to the ground and dies, it remains a single seed. But if it dies, it produces many seeds." It is only as we are broken that we can go on to become what God designed for us to be. This is something everyone has to deal with no matter how committed we are to God. We have to die to ourselves and our goals and dreams and put Christ first in our lives.

There was a time in my life when I felt God had taken everything away from me. I was 31 years old. My husband and I were living about 700 miles away from home. Things were going well, and then out of nowhere, I lost my job. A few weeks later we found out that the church we had been trying to help start was not going to make it. The pastor moved out of state and the congregation disbanded. Then a few weeks later I had a miscarriage. So within a two-month window, just about everything I valued had been taken away from me. I had been so involved in work and church that the only people I knew were in one of those two places.

Now I found myself alone and grieving the loss of a child. I had to make a decision. Who was I going to trust to put the pieces back together, myself or God? I went through a short period of time where I questioned God and wondered what he was doing and why he was doing it.

What I grew to realize was that God had taken me to a point where I had to be completely dependent on him. There was nothing else left. He used this time in my life to break my pride and self-reliance. Then when I turned to him, he picked me up and loved me and my faith grew.

Remember that God's purpose for us is not for us to simply live a comfortable lifestyle. His purpose is to mature us in our walk with him so that we can be effective witnesses for the kingdom.

The idea of brokenness is hard for us to understand. It is so countercultural. Our society screams, "be all that you can be." Brokenness says be what God has created you to be. Society tells us to "live in the moment." Brokenness teaches us to live with our eyes on eternity. Society says "have it your way." Brokenness says there's no other way but God's way. Society teaches us instant gratification. We get everything fast. Microwave ovens cook our food fast. Credit cards allow us to purchase things without saving the money. This is the opposite of what God wants for us. Brokenness is a process that takes time. We don't become broken and get over it in a day.

I am reminded of how God took Moses into the desert for 40 years in order to break him and prepare him for the task he had ahead of him. Forty years is a long time to be in brokenness. What was God teaching him? He was teaching Moses to totally trust him. Moses lost everything that he knew. He lost his family, his home, his privileges, his standing, his power, and his pride. Remember he was being raised as a child of the Pharaoh and now all of a sudden he was in a desert tending sheep. He was used to having servants do all his work for him and now he was doing all the physical labor himself. He was bringing Moses to the place where he was ready to fully rely on God and was willing to do whatever God asked him to do. Finally, Moses was ready to accomplish what God had planned for him in leading the Israelites out of Egypt.[2]

We tend to resist the process of brokenness. It's hard to give up our goals and plans for our lives. We don't understand brokenness. We are afraid of it. It's hard to enter into the unknown but that's where Jesus is. He draws us. He calls us. He longs for us to come to him. He wants to heal us. We have to quit striving and trying to fix things on our own. We have to recognize our need for God and focus on him. That is where true healing comes from for us. Only when we admit our need to God, can he use the situations in our lives to make us what he created us to be. We have to let go of our ego, pride, and independent spirit and put God in the center of our lives. These are choices we make as an act of our will. When we resist, we hinder our relationship with God, and we limit how God can use us.

Do you remember the story of the women with the alabaster jar from Luke 7? Jesus was invited to have dinner with one of the Pharisees. A woman, who was known to be sinful, found out where Jesus was going to be, and she came there with an alabaster jar of perfume. She broke the jar and poured the perfume on Jesus. She understood brokenness. She had to break the jar, the most valuable thing she owned, to give the perfume to Jesus. She had been through some tough times in her life. She had been despised and rejected and then she met Jesus. It broke her to know that Jesus loved her, as he loves each of us.

The Pharisee didn't understand what was going on. He thought what she did was a waste. He could only see the physical realm of this event. He couldn't see the spiritual significance.

Inside each of us is something of value, and God wants to break us so that it can come out. We must allow ourselves to be broken, and poured out at the feet of Jesus. Our lives are a sweet aroma that God can use. The only wasted fragrance is the one that stays sealed up in the bottle.

Here are a few things that we need to remember. God allows us to be broken because he sees the potential in our lives. He wants to bring out our best. He wants to bless us. God loves us too much to allow us to live in sin. He loves us too much to allow us remain stagnant in our Christian walk. His love for us motivates him to mature us. He longs to see us in a deep relationship with him and in an effective ministry for him.

When you are going through a period of brokenness, ask God to reveal to you what he is doing in your life. What does he desire for you to do as a result of your brokenness? Ask yourself if there is anything that you are holding on to that would keep you from experiencing God's best for your life. Nothing in this world compares to what God's got planned for you. Don't run from brokenness; embrace it. God's going to use it in your life for your benefit and his glory.

For further thought:

"The Lord is close to the brokenhearted and saves those who are crushed in spirit." (Psalm 34:18)

"But seek first his kingdom and his righteousness, and all these things will be given to you as well." (Matthew 6:33)

"And we know that in all things God works for the good of those who love him, who have been called according to his purpose." (Romans 8:28)

"I have been crucified with Christ and I no longer live, but Christ lives in me. The life I now live in the body, I live by faith in the Son of God, who loved me and gave himself for me." (Galatians 2:20)

4 THE STORM OF BUSYNESS

Life is busy and it seems to keep getting busier. Busy has become the default state of my life and, as a result of that, I am constantly exhausted. I am under pressure at work and at home. The pace of life is incredible, and time is something that I always seem to lack. My to-do list is never ending. As fast as I get the house cleaned, it needs it again. Then there's the laundry, is it ever done? If I just had more time…

Time is something God gives equally to all people. We all get 365 days in a year, seven days in a week, and 24 hours in a day. No one gets any more or any less. Each day has 1440 minutes and 86,400 seconds. Nothing can change that. No one can get any more. We can't buy more. We can't negotiate for more. Once we've used a minute, we can't get it back. It's gone forever. There aren't any "do overs."

How we spend our time is something we have control over. I believe we can tell what is important to people by how they spend their time. Work is a given for most of us. It steals a large portion of our days. So here's a hint, we should do something we love. Hopefully some of the rest of our time would be spent on things like family, friends, and God.

I was recently thinking about the story of Mary and Martha that comes from Luke 10. Mary sat at Jesus' feet and listened to him speak. Her eyes and heart were fixed on him. Her heart was open to his voice. She simply sat at his feet and worshipped. Martha was very worried about taking care of all the work and preparations. She was so consumed with what needed to be done, that she missed the point of Jesus' visit.

It is easy for me to relate to Martha. She is busy serving, helping, and doing good stuff. She's not lazy; she's a worker. But in her efforts to serve, she missed what was most important. I can also relate to Mary. I long to sit at Jesus' feet. However, the daily demands of this life make that difficult. And so, it means I need to make that time in my schedule a priority. There is a balance that needs to be found between working and worship. Both are important, but neither should outweigh the other. There are lots of times I feel like I'm not godly enough, not doing enough, not serving others enough, etc. Many times I get too serious, and I don't enjoy the day the Lord has given me. I'm going through life but not really living.

Often the commitments that I take on that are part of "God's work" are the things that put me over the edge. When it comes to church activities and serving God, I just can't say "no." Then before I know it, I've taken on too much and my schedule is running my life. Obviously, serving God is a good thing. But I need to assess the responsibilities I have, what I'm being asked to add, and really consider if I can handle more. Otherwise, I try to do too much and busyness affects the way I function as a wife, mother, daughter, friend, and employee. I get stressed out and even resentful of the time commitments that some activities require. I lose the ability to have a servant's heart and I just feel tired, worn-out, and frustrated.

I think busyness is one of the devil's schemes. He tries to get me off-track. He tries to get me to waste the time God has given me. He tries to keep me busy with religious activities so I won't have time to really connect with the living God. He tries to get my mind to wander and not to engage with God. I need to focus on God's love for me and my love for him. When I love someone, I delight in what he delights in. It's easy to serve someone I love. It's easy to spend time with someone I love.

I need to focus on strengthening my connection with God. That can happen anywhere and anytime, and everywhere and all the time. It's not a ritual, it's a relationship. Just like any other relationship in my life, it takes time to build it and maintain it. What I need to learn is that I am satisfied only as I rest in him. As I rest in him, life has less stress and more joy.

I want to grow in my faith so that I am more like Mary. I want the faith to be able to rest and not be anxious. I want the wisdom to see what is most important. I want faith to trust God to provide and to be able to simply sit at his feet and worship him. How do I get there? What do I need to change? Perhaps I need to examine exactly what it is that is keeping me busy. Is there a way for me to spend my time more wisely? Time is a precious gift from God and it is to be guarded. I do not know how old I will live to be, but I do know that each and every day has a finite number of hours. I need to guard those hours. I need to not just go through life, but really live it and experience it.

If you are living an overly-busy lifestyle today, then perhaps the Lord is calling you to make some changes. Spend some time in his presence and in his Word, and let him teach you how to order your days. Let him give you hope, purpose, and peace.

For further thought:

"Why, you do not even know what will happen tomorrow. What is your life? You are a mist that appears for a little while and then vanishes." (James 4:14)

"Man is like a mere breath; his days are like a passing shadow." (Psalm 144:4)

"Be still, and know that I am God." (Psalm 46:10)

"Be very careful, then, how you live - not as unwise but as wise, making the most of every opportunity, because the days are evil." (Ephesians 5:15-16)

5 THE STORM OF DISCOURAGEMENT

Have you ever been discouraged? I don't think anyone can honestly answer "no." I've had times in my life when I have been discouraged. Things didn't work out the way I planned. I didn't get a job or a raise I thought I deserved. Rehab after a surgery took longer than I thought it would. There have been times when I have prayed earnestly for something and it didn't happen.

Why do we get discouraged? Sometimes it actually comes from a physical cause. When we are tired and worn out, it is easier to get discouraged. Sometimes we just have unrealistic goals or expectations. It can easily come when we let our focus slip off of God and onto ourselves. We find we aren't trusting God to take care of us and things in our lives.

Some people deal with discouragement by plunging themselves into things they think will bring them pleasure. Things like sports, traveling, or their career. Others turn to drugs, alcohol, or adultery. None of these things will take away the discouragement. In fact, they will only take them deeper into discouragement.

So where do we go for help? There are several things I can think of that help us overcome discouragement. The first is to go to the Word of God. We should spend time there renewing our minds and refreshing our souls. We need to hear God speak to us through his Word. When we are discouraged, this may seem like the last thing we want to do, but it is the thing we must do. We must guard against our feelings, and see what God has to say.

I remember one particular time I was really struggling. I was recovering from wrist surgery and was going to the doctor's office to get my stitches removed. I was expecting a splint, as that was what the doctor had indicated was the usual next step. However, that was not what happened. After examining the wrist, he felt it was best to put it into a cast for two more weeks. I was ready for the splint. I had myself prepared for that. I desperately wanted to shower without putting a bag over my arm. I was discouraged and frustrated. I had already endured surgery, a cast, a splint, rehab, cortisone shots, and then another surgery. This process had taken over 21 months, and I was ready to be finished. Now I got a two-week delay. Two weeks doesn't sound like a lot, but I had been counting the days until I got the use of my arm back. How does one handle discouragement and frustration like this? I tried to be patient. I tried to remind myself that there are lots of people in the world who are worse off than I was. I tried giving myself a pep talk. None of that seemed to work.

When I went home that day, I opened my Bible and started reading through Hebrews 11 and 12. It contains some of my favorite verses. Hebrews 11 is the great chapter on faith. The chapter ends by talking about the sufferings of the Jewish people. Some of those things were mockings, scourgings, chains, imprisonments, stonings, being sawed in two, temptations, death by the sword, and homelessness. Ok – I get it. They were definitely worse off than me. Then I looked at chapter 12. It is written to give discouraged Christians hope. The writer describes being surrounded by a great cloud of witnesses - those who have gone before us who, despite their struggles, have remained true to their faith.

> Therefore, since we are surrounded by such a great cloud of witnesses, let us throw off everything that hinders and the sin that so easily entangles, and let us run with perseverance the race marked out for us. Let us fix our eyes on Jesus, the author and perfecter of our faith, who for the joy set before him endured the cross, scorning its shame, and sat down at the right hand of the throne of God. (Hebrews 12:1-2)

Try to picture what this says. First we are told to "throw off everything that hinders." This makes me think of a big load that I am supposed to put down. What am I carrying around every day that I really don't need? Am shouldering burdens that I need to entrust to God? Next, I am to get rid of "the sin that so easily entangles." The word *entangles* makes me think that the devil is trying to confuse me, catch me, and ruin my walk with Christ. The devil would do anything to trip me up and get me off on the wrong path. Then I am to "run with perseverance the race."

The word *perseverance* implies patience and consistency. I am picturing a runner in a race. He has gotten rid of everything that could possibly weigh him down. He is watching every step, so as to avoid any sinful traps. He runs with hope, patience, and consistency. How does he do all this? The next verse gives the answer. The way to accomplish this is by focusing on Jesus. Keep your eyes on Jesus.

If I am focusing all my attention on Jesus, I should know three things. The first is – *Who is Jesus?* "The author and perfecter of our faith" He is the originator, writer, creator, and the captain of my faith. He is the starting point for my faith, and he controls my faith. Without Jesus, I have no faith. When it says he is the perfecter of my faith, that means he is the finisher and the sustainer of my faith. I have complete confidence that he will finish what he started in me.

The second thing to know is – *What did Jesus do?* "endured the cross, scorning its shame" He suffered more than I ever will. He knows what it is like to be mocked, scorned, beaten, forgotten, deserted, etc. There is no frustration I can go through that will ever compare to what he has already endured.

The third thing is - *Where is Jesus now?* - "sat down at the right hand of the throne of God." Jesus is sitting next to God in a position of power and authority.

Hebrews 7:25 states, "Therefore he is able to save completely those who come to God through him, because he always lives to intercede for them."

This means that I can keep on keeping on because Jesus is in the presence of God, constantly pleading for me. Thank God that when I am frustrated, disappointed, and discouraged, he is there praying for me and carrying me through it.

So going back to my story - as I went through the next two weeks, time passed quickly. Before I knew it, it was time to take the cast off and go back to rehab and ultimately get the use of my arm back. God does that for us. As we focus on him, he encourages us and allows us to endure the hard times.

Another thing we can do to help overcome discouragement is to get busy serving the Lord. One of the causes of discouragement is that we become too focused on ourselves. That can lead to us to quit serving the Lord. In 1 Kings 19, Elijah was worn out from his struggles to defeat Jezebel and her prophets of Baal. He was so depressed that he cried out to God to end his life.

"I have had enough, LORD," he said. "Take my life; I am no better than my ancestors" (1 Kings 19:4b).

This kind of self-focus keeps us from seeing the needs of others and serving them. What did God do with Elijah? He told him to get up, eat, and get going. Get back to working for the Lord.

One final thought in overcoming discouragement is simply *trust God*. Paul says in Philippians 1:6 that "he who began a good work in you will carry it on to completion until the day of Christ Jesus." We can trust God to complete his work in us.

So when those discouraging days come, get in the Word and allow God to teach you, look for someone to whom you can reach out, and trust God to get you through. He'll never let you down.

For further thought:

"Trust in the LORD with all your heart and lean not on your own understanding; in all your ways submit to him, and he will make your paths straight." (Proverbs 3:5-6)

"So do not fear, for I am with you; do not be dismayed, for I am your God. I will strengthen you and help you; I will uphold you with my righteous right hand." (Isaiah 41:10)

"And let us not grow weary of doing good, for in due season we will reap, if we do not give up." (Galatians 6:9)

"For our light and momentary troubles are achieving for us an eternal glory that far outweighs them all. So we fix our eyes not on what is seen, but on what is unseen, since what is seen is temporary, but what is unseen is eternal." (2 Corinthians 4:17-18)

6 THE STORM OF DOUBT

This is one of the topics that hits closest home with me. However, I may not be thinking about doubt in the same way that you do. I think of this as honestly questioning your faith, more of being skeptical not cynical. Ok - so what's the difference? A skeptic has reservations. He is not easily convinced. He needs to be persuaded. A cynic believes the worst and distrusts. A skeptic knows there are bad people in the world, and he is careful. A cynic knows there are bad people in the world, and therefore assumes everyone is bad.

I think doubt is something that almost every Christian experiences at some point, and I also think doubt is healthy. It causes us to question things that we've been told all our lives and makes us seek and find answers for ourselves. Acts 17:11 says, "Now the Berean Jews were of more noble character than those in Thessalonica, for they received the message with great eagerness and examined the scriptures every day to see if what Paul said was true." They weren't satisfied to know that Paul said it. They wanted to know that what Paul said matched what God said.

Asking questions is a healthy part of a growing faith. It means our faith is alive. It doesn't help to ignore doubts or to feel guilty about them. Many Christians actually hide behind their doubts. They are afraid to let others know they have questions. It is in searching the scriptures, seeking God, and honestly dealing with issues, that we develop a deep-rooted faith. That is one that isn't easily shaken. Sadly, many Christians are afraid to look closely at their own faith. They are like the disciples who watched Peter step out of the boat and onto the waves. They are thinking, *you just can't do that. It's dangerous.*

If we have never doubted anything, then we have never really thought seriously about it. The only way to never doubt is to never use our minds. I would say it would be hard to mature in our Christian faith without ever having any doubts. If doubting wasn't possible, then one wouldn't need faith. Doubting does not mean we don't have faith, but rather it means we are trying to take our faith to a deeper level. We must not be afraid to doubt. It will take us to a more thorough understanding of the character of God.

Honest doubting means we are seeking understanding. Simple answers don't satisfy. Just because my parents believed it is no longer an acceptable answer. Honest doubt makes us seek to know and to comprehend truth. Honest doubt makes us want to know more about God and experience him in new ways. I think God honors our struggles to apprehend truth. I'm not sure God is as excited about someone who just passively believes everything he is told. We must engage God, fight with him, and not just blindly believe everything we hear. I am reminded of Jacob who wrestled with God. God won the wrestling match but Jacob came away a changed man (Genesis 32).

God desires us to be a people who will ask, seek, and knock (Matthew 7:7). We've got to be willing to do something. It is in questioning that we gain understanding. Our relationship with God is too important for us not to struggle with. We may question things, but then pray, read, study, think, talk to others, and wrestle it through until we come out with an answer, one that we are sure is from God. But also know that we will never have all the answers. While it is important to seek answers, some questions will remain forever. God is infinitely bigger, better, wiser, and more knowledgeable than we are. And so faith and doubt is really a paradox. Where does one stop and the other start? "Without faith it is impossible to please God" (Hebrews 11:6). Faith involves taking risks. If we have to have all the answers, we will never have faith.

Let's look at the life of Thomas. I think Thomas got a bad rap. I don't think he deserved the stigma of being called a doubter. Remember the story - Jesus was dead. People were scattering. They were disappointed and confused. They heard him proclaim his deity. They thought he was going to actually establish a physical kingdom and rule the earth.

How could Jesus walk on water, perform many, many miracles, and yet not stop his own murder? Some of the disciples even thought their journey was over. Peter gave into the pressure and denied Jesus three times. Then something happened. The tomb was empty. Dozens of people were proclaiming to have seen Jesus. The disciples rallied together. They arranged a meeting in the upper room. They spent hours discussing what they had seen. Many had encountered Jesus on the road to Emmaus. Others saw the empty tomb and the burial clothes that Jesus left behind. Everything was going great ... and then Thomas spoke up.

Thomas had heard all the stories but just couldn't believe all of this to be true. Thomas had to see Jesus for himself and actually touch him before he was going to believe again. What happened next? Jesus appeared. Thomas got his eye-witness account. Thomas got what he needed to believe. Thomas didn't really care to hear the testimonies of others. He wanted his own experience.

Let's try to look at him from a different perspective. Thomas was on a search for the truth. He didn't want second-hand knowledge. He wanted to personally know Jesus was alive. He didn't want to live the rest of his life on someone else's faith and experience.[1]

Therefore, perhaps his doubt came from a desire to be sure, not from disbelief. Maybe Thomas was merely protecting his heart from being broken again. After all, Thomas had enough faith to go to the upper room with the other disciples. He didn't turn his back and run away. Thomas was on a search for truth, and Jesus knew that and helped him.

Christianity is filled with people whose faith is based on someone else's experience. Their belief is not necessarily their conviction but may be based simply on the way they were raised or on their culture. We need more Thomases in the church. We need people who aren't content to live out their beliefs on the basis of other people's relationship with Christ. We need people who possess their own faith and whose trust in God is personal.

How did the story of Thomas end? Thomas traveled to India as a missionary and died there as a martyr. Today the church in India is still alive and well. Thomas' doubt turned into a radical commitment to live and die for Christ.[2]

For further thought:

"But when he asks, he must believe and not doubt, because he who doubts is like a wave of the sea, blown and tossed by the wind. That man should not think he will receive anything from the Lord; he is a double-minded man, unstable in all he does." (James 1:6-8)

"Then he said to Thomas, 'Put your finger here; see my hands. Reach out your hand and put it into my side. Stop doubting and believe.'" (John 20:27)

"And without faith it is impossible to please God, because anyone who comes to him must believe that he exists and that he rewards those who earnestly seek him." (Hebrews 11:6)

7 THE STORM OF FEAR

Fear is an emotion that can cripple a person. Fear can be displayed as worry, guilt, stress, depression, confusion, etc. The main kinds of fear are that of death, sickness, failure, and rejection. Should a Christian be fearful? John 10:10 says, "The thief comes only to steal and kill and destroy; I have come that they may have life, and have it to the full." The devil loves to operate through fear. Is fear really a lack of trust? The Bible tells us that fear doesn't come from God. Paul writes in 2 Timothy 1:7, "For God has not given us a spirit of fear, but of power and love and of a sound mind."

So how do we conquer the fear in our lives? I think we do it by knowing and using the Word of God. When the devil tempted Jesus, Jesus simply quoted scripture.

I recently went through a very difficult time in my life; one that no woman should ever have to go through. I became fearful of a lot of things. One exercise that I used that proved to be helpful to me was I simply made a list in my journal of everything I was fearful of and then one-by-one I prayed through the list and surrendered it to God.[1] Everyone's list is different. Some of the things on my list included:

- I was afraid that I would be alone.
- I was afraid that my marriage would fail.
- I was afraid that I'd never feel safe again.
- I was afraid that I'd look like a fool for trying to keep it together.
- I was afraid that my emotions would never feel in balance again.
- I was afraid that the pain I was experiencing would never end.
- I was afraid that my heart would never feel the same.
- I was afraid that I would never feel strong again.
- I was afraid that I would never trust again.

I asked God to help me release all my fears and to help me trust him completely. I asked him to take my situation and work it for good. Then I just began to claim scripture verses like:

So do not fear, for I am with you; do not be dismayed, for I am your God. I will strengthen you and help you; I will uphold you with my righteous right hand. (Isaiah 41:10)

And we know that in all things God works for the good of those who love him, who have been called according to his purpose. (Romans 8:28)

"For I know the plans I have for you," declares the LORD, "plans to prosper you and not to harm you, plans to give you hope and a future." (Jeremiah 29:11)

But he said to me, "My grace is sufficient for you, for my power is made perfect in weakness." (2 Corinthians 12:9)

When facing fear, what we allow our minds to dwell on is extremely important. Romans 12:2 tells us to be transformed by the renewing of our minds. How do we do that? I think we start with what Paul said in 2 Corinthians 10:5, "we take captive every thought to make it obedient to Christ." We must be careful with every single thought and be purposeful about what we spend our time thinking. Don't let our minds dwell on the things that cause us fear, hurt, or pain. In the book of Philippians, Paul gives us some direction:

Finally, brothers and sisters, whatever is true, whatever is noble, whatever is right, whatever is pure, whatever is lovely, whatever is admirable - if anything is excellent or praiseworthy - think about such things. (Philippians 4:8)

Paul tells us if we focus our thoughts on these things, then we will have peace.

Many Christians think that if they are living right, nothing will come into their lives that will make them feel afraid. They say things like, "Doesn't God want me to be happy?" Actually, God is not all that concerned with our happiness. He gives us joy that comes from a close relationship with him. However, he never tells us that circumstances in our lives will not cause us stress, pain, and fear. In fact, it is in these difficult circumstances that our faith grows.

Romans 5 says that suffering produces perseverance, perseverance, character, and character, hope. I know in my own life, the difficult times are the ones that forced me to my knees seeking God. It was in these times that I grew in my faith.

The key to not being afraid is to totally trust God. We need to trust God with such a strong resolve that there's no way we will give in to fear. We must turn to God in our hard times and trust him to make things right. Where does this kind of trust come from? It comes from knowing who God is. We should spend some time really studying the attributes of the God that we serve. When we understand who our loving heavenly Father is, we will also understand that we have no need to fear.

Spend some time thinking about what causes you fear. Don't allow uncontrolled fear to interfere with your relationship with Christ. Remember that Jesus died to set you free from fear. Jesus wants to help you through all the fearful circumstances of your life. You have a choice to make. Trust God and not be afraid, or be afraid and not trust God. Which will you choose?

For further thought:

"There is no fear in love. But perfect love drives out fear, because fear has to do with punishment." (1 John 4:18)

"The LORD is my light and my salvation - whom shall I fear?
The LORD is the stronghold of my life - of whom shall I be afraid?" (Psalm 27:1)

"So we say with confidence, 'The Lord is my helper; I will not be afraid. What can mere mortals do to me?' " (Hebrews 13:66)

"I sought the LORD, and he answered me; he delivered me from all my fears." (Psalm 34:4)

8 THE STORM OF GRUMPINESS

Have you ever seen the sign or T-shirt that says, "Sometimes I wake up Grumpy and sometimes I let him sleep"? Perhaps that is a description of you. Why are some people grumpy and others joyful?

I'm typically a pretty upbeat person, but even I can get up on the wrong side of the bed sometimes. When that happens, I try to analyze why and it usually comes down to two things. I either overslept and now have to rush, or I didn't sleep enough last night and I am exhausted. Sometimes both of those can happen in the same morning!

One particular grumpy morning, I had overslept by about 30 minutes. It was not enough to be late for work, but enough that I had to rush, and I had to skip my quiet time. I try hard to spend some time with God each morning before leaving for work. Acknowledging his presence in my life and allowing him to enter the day with me helps me get my day off to a good start. So instead of having time to read for a few minutes and pray, I was rushing around getting ready. The whole morning was filled with rushing and grumping. And exactly who was I angry with? It was my own fault that I overslept. So I got to work and threw myself into the day. One of the first things I had to do was get my email. Of course, that was the day when Outlook froze on my computer, and I had to shut it down and try again. Then another problem popped up, and soon I found myself having to reboot my entire computer. I was frustrated and grumpy, and now I was getting behind in my work.

Then the Lord started to work on my heart. Things go wrong, but that doesn't mean I should let them affect my attitude. I really didn't want to take my frustrations out on anyone else. I wasn't angry with anyone. I was just frustrated. However, I knew if anyone came in my office that morning, they weren't going to see Christ shining out through my life. They were going to see someone who resembled the Wicked Witch of the West. I knew I needed an attitude adjustment and quick. Constant complaining or whining makes me lose focus on the truth that God is good. I know that God continues to bless me time and time again, but my attitude that morning wasn't one of gratefulness.

Numbers 14 talks about how the children of Israel complained.

> That night all the members of the community raised their voices and wept aloud. All the Israelites grumbled against Moses and Aaron, and the whole assembly said to them, "If only we had died in Egypt! Or in this wilderness!" (Numbers 14:1-2)

They didn't see that their constant complaining was having a negative impact on their relationship with God. Their complaining showed a lack of trust in God's provision for them. Their bad attitudes actually changed God's plan and prevented them from entering the Promised Land.

When we complain, we run the risk of neutralizing the power of God in our lives as well. To insist on being a negative, grumpy, whiny person will eventually cost us our intimacy with the Father. We don't have to be like the Israelites. We can make a choice to change our attitude.

Going back to my story, I took a few minutes and paused and prayed. I asked God to help me overcome my "grumps." I knew that I was going to be interacting with people, and I wanted them to see Christ living in me. I have been fairly outspoken at work about my faith, and I didn't want to ruin my testimony. I really desire to be "salt and light," and I knew that I couldn't be those in my current mental state. As I prayed and confessed my bad attitude to God, he changed my heart. I asked him to help me rejoice in all things, to help me trust him, and to help me count my blessings. It didn't take long, but it sure did make a difference.

We must not be afraid to admit to God when we have a bad attitude. He knows it anyway and he's waiting to help us and encourage us.

For further thought:

"If we claim to be without sin, we deceive ourselves and the truth is not in us. If we confess our sins, he is faithful and just and will forgive us our sins and purify us from all unrighteousness." (1 John 1:8-9)

"Do everything without grumbling or arguing, so that you may become blameless and pure, 'children of God without fault in a warped and crooked generation.' Then you will shine among them like stars in the sky." (Philippians 2:14-15)

"Rejoice in the Lord always. I will say it again: Rejoice!" (Philippians 4:4)

9 THE STORM OF BETRAYAL

Have you ever been betrayed? Perhaps a friend broke a confidence. Maybe a spouse wasn't faithful. Perhaps someone gossiped about you or lied about you. A trust was broken. A secret was told. Someone wasn't loyal to you. All of these are examples of betrayal.

A friend of mine experienced this kind of betrayal and the pain from it was real, deep, and long lasting. It wasn't an easy thing for her to get over. Her first reaction when trust was broken was one of shock. She wasn't expecting this to happen. She found it hard to believe that someone she loved actually repaid her love by breaking her trust. It was almost impossible for her to comprehend that someone she had been committed to for a long period of time could destroy their relationship this way. After she got over the shock, the pain sunk in. She was left with the feeling that perhaps their relationship was beyond repair. She never expected it, and yet she realized that if the relationship was going to be healed, it was going to take a long time. She no longer trusted this person. She no longer wanted to openly share her heart. She guarded every step she took, and every word she spoke. She was left in a defensive position just trying to protect herself from future pain. This was an exhausting place to be. It was a constant emotional drain. She wondered if it was worth the time and the effort.

Restoring trust after a betrayal can take years of time and a lot of effort. Some people work on it, and others determine it just isn't worth the effort. Pride can get in the way. The offender may not want to admit he was wrong. He also might not want to change the behavior that caused the problem. Pride was also a factor on her part. She had been hurt so deeply that she didn't want to forgive easily. Shouldn't he have to pay for what he put her through? Eventually she understood that she needed to forgive, and that the person she was most hurting by not forgiving him was herself. She couldn't move on and heal as long as she had an unforgiving spirit. That unforgiving spirit also affected her relationship with her heavenly Father. By not forgiving this person, she was telling God that this offense against her was more important than her relationship with God.

Forgiving a person who wronged you is one thing, but ever trusting him again, that's a whole different matter. Nothing shakes your confidence in someone more than finding out you can't trust him. You don't want to be around him. You don't want to talk to him. Just the sight of that person can make you sick to your stomach, because you remember how badly you've been hurt. The relationship will never be the same. You might be able to get past the wrong that's been done, but you can never undo it and go back to the way you were before.

It was comforting to her to know that Jesus understood exactly what she was going through. He handpicked his disciples. He lived with them, ate with them, trained them, and did life with them for three years. He loved them, and he trusted them. Then one of his own, Judas, betrayed him. What did Judas get for his betrayal? Thirty pieces of silver. Jesus felt the pain of this betrayal, and it cost him his life.

Peter also betrayed Jesus. I have to think this one might actually have hurt Jesus more than Judas' action. Jesus loved Peter and saw great potential in Peter. Yet on the night Jesus was arrested, Peter denied knowing him three times. Jesus still loved Peter even after the betrayal, and he still believed in him. After Jesus' death and resurrection, he actually reinstated Peter. You know the story from John 21. Three times Jesus asked Peter if he loved him, and all three times Peter responded that he did. Jesus told him, "Feed my sheep." Jesus not only forgave Peter, but he built him back up and encouraged him. Peter rose up, regained his confidence, and went on to do great things for God.

As I thought some more about these ideas, I realized that I too have betrayed Jesus. How? I've had divided affections. I've had times in my life when I've placed work, family, and even self before God. I've desired things more than God. I've had times when I should have spoken up for God, and I've stayed silent. I've had opportunities to share about what Christ has done for me, and I kept quiet. I've lacked passion in pursuing my relationship with Christ. I've ignored him for days at a time. I've made decisions without consulting his Word. All of these are examples of betrayal. And so I also betrayed Jesus, the one who loved me so much that he willingly gave up his life for me.

So where does that leave me? That leaves me at the feet of Jesus asking for forgiveness. Forgiveness for myself, my actions, my attitudes, and my betrayal. It also leaves me asking Jesus to help restore the broken relationships in my life. Help to give me the hope that I need to have that restoration is possible. Help me be forgiving and encouraging.

What do you need help from Jesus with today?

For further thought:

"And when you stand praying, if you hold anything against anyone, forgive them, so that your Father in heaven may forgive you your sins." (Mark 11:25)

"Do not repay anyone evil for evil. Be careful to do what is right in the eyes of everyone. If it is possible, as far as it depends on you, live at peace with everyone. Do not take revenge, my dear friends, but leave room for God's wrath, for it is written: 'It is mine to avenge; I will repay,' says the Lord." (Romans 12:17-19)

"Jesus replied: 'Love the Lord your God with all your heart and with all your soul and with all your mind.' This is the first and greatest commandment. And the second is like it: 'Love your neighbor as yourself.' " (Matthew 22:37-39)

10 THE STORM OF MOURNING (GRIEF)

As I am writing this, I am still grieving over the loss of my best friend. It's been less than a month since she died. She died completely unexpectedly, and her death caught me completely off-guard. I am not sad for her. She simply beat me to heaven. I am sad, because I have to remain here without her.

Grief is a natural healthy response to pain and loss. There is nothing wrong with grieving. It is part of the healing process. Solomon wrote in Ecclesiastes chapter 3 that there is a time for everything, "a time to be born and a time to die."

Death is a part of life. In fact, I've heard it said that from the moment we are born, we are on a journey to our death. Some get to the end of the journey faster than others. We all die. That's a biological fact. The only thing we don't know is when and how death will occur.

In John 11, we read the story about when Lazarus died. Jesus went to the town of Bethany, where Lazarus was buried. He saw Martha and the others mourning, and he was so moved by their grief that he also wept. This is interesting, because he knew he was going to raise Lazarus from the dead, and yet he took part in the grief process.

Grief can help us gain perspective on life. It has a purpose, but it is also just for a season. David wrote in Psalm 30 that "weeping may stay for the night, but rejoicing comes in the morning" (Psalm 30:5b). God sees our tears and knows our hearts. He is always there beside us to get us through the hard times. Our part is to "be still" and rest in the knowledge that the God of the universe loves us unconditionally and is completely sovereign over every situation. Nothing can touch us without God allowing it to happen.

It is important that we express our grief to God. As I was reading through the Psalms, I noticed that many of the Psalms start with the psalmist pouring out his heart to God, but by the time you get to the end of the Psalm, his attitude has turned into praise.

When we talk with the Lord and keep our hearts soft toward him, he reminds us how much he loves us. He reminds us that he has a plan in everything. He reminds us that he is faithful, and that we can trust him.

I will continue through life now without my best friend and that reminds me of how much I need the body of Christ. We hold each other up in the tough times of life. I need that right now. Grief is a part of life. We must never forget that we have hope in Christ. We know he is strong enough to carry our burdens. We know that he cares for us (I Peter 5:7).

What to do now ...

- Cast all my burdens on him.
- As a body of believers, comfort one another.
- Stay in the Word, and allow God to speak to my heart.
- Rest in the hope of salvation.

For further thought:

"Jesus said to her, "I am the resurrection and the life. The one who believes in me will live, even though they die." (John 11:25)

"Do not let your hearts be troubled. You believe in God; believe also in me. My Father's house has many rooms; if that were not so, would I have told you that I am going there to prepare a place for you? And if I go and prepare a place for you, I will come back and take you to be with me that you also may be where I am. You know the way to the place where I am going." (John 14:1-4)

"Praise be to the God and Father of our Lord Jesus Christ, the Father of compassion and the God of all comfort, who comforts us in all our troubles, so that we can comfort those in any trouble with the comfort we ourselves receive from God." (2 Corinthians 1:3-4)

11 THE STORM OF DISTRACTIONS

I work in the field of technology. Multitasking is my norm. Having an uninterrupted conversation with anyone is sometimes difficult. Phone calls, text messages, and to-do lists are constantly taking priority in my life. It is rare to be able to look someone in the eye without interruption or distraction. Recently I found myself, talking on my phone, emailing on my laptop, and trying to hold a conversation with my daughter all at the same time. She deserves better than that. She deserves my full attention. She needs her Mom to really listen. In my quest to accomplish a lot, I lost focus on what was important.

This same kind of problem can affect my spiritual life. I sometimes find it hard to simply be with God. I have a hard time focusing only on him. I struggle putting everything else out of my mind. I try not to multitask, but to give him my undivided attention. I try to get alone, and "be still" before the Lord. It is hard for me to close out everything around me. No music, no phone, no TV, no computer, etc. It is takes discipline to intentionally take myself away from all of these things, and focus on prayer and Bible study.

Did Jesus have to deal with distractions? It is true that he didn't have to deal with emails or texts. However, he had multitudes of people constantly pursuing him. Yet, he knew how to make his relationship with the Father a priority. He looked for and found ways to escape. He took time to focus and be quiet (Mark 1:35). He was willing to do whatever it took to remove himself from the demands of the people and find a spot to pray. Our lack of intimacy is often due to our refusal to unplug from technology. We must make a conscious effort to shut off communication from others in order to focus on our relationship with God.

In the crazy world, it takes tremendous effort to find a quiet place. It takes a commitment to purposefully block out time in my schedule and dedicate it to my relationship with God. I need time to get quiet before the Lord. Sometimes it means going to a different location so that I can focus. It will look different for different people, but being quiet before the Lord is the goal. As I try to make this time a priority in my schedule, I have been tempted to cut it short or even eliminate it on some days. I must not give in. I need to stand firm in my commitment to be still, to listen, and to cut out the distractions of the world. As I practice this stillness, I experience deep intimacy with the Father.

God said to Israel, "You will seek me and find me, when you seek me with all your heart. I will be found by you, declares the Lord" (Jeremiah 29:13-14).

When is the last time you sought after God with all your heart? God still desires to be sought and found by his people. So try this: quiet your mind, quiet your heart, focus on God, focus on his love for you, and focus on his faithfulness. Pray and ask God to help you set aside time (and everything else), so that you can seek him with your whole heart.

For further thought:

"Tremble and do not sin; when you are on your beds, search your hearts and be silent." (Psalm 4:4)

"Be still, and know that I am God." (Psalm 46:10)

"But they who wait for the Lord shall renew their strength; they shall mount up with wings like eagles; they shall run and not be weary; they shall walk and not faint." (Isaiah 40:31)

12 THE STORM OF LONELINESS

Loneliness affects lots of people. As we look at the idea of loneliness, it is important to define what we mean by that term. Loneliness is not the same as solitude or isolation. Loneliness can take place when we are alone or when we are in a crowd of people. It can be at home or when we are out. It can happen on special days or just ordinary days. There really are no rules. It's a sense of not being wanted, not being necessary, not having anyone with whom to share our hearts.

Loneliness is something I struggled with after the death of my best friend. We had been friends for 40 years, and God decided to take her home at the young age of 53. We had lots in common and shared just about everything with each other. She knew things about me that I wouldn't dream of telling anyone else. She was more than my best friend. She was like a sister to me. When she died, I felt like a piece of me died as well. I had no one to talk to, laugh with, cry with, play with, run around with, or simply "be" with. I could share things with her without fear of judgment or ridicule. She could take a bad situation and make me look at it from a completely different angle, and pretty soon it didn't seem so overwhelming. I missed her greatly, and therefore, I was lonely.

Have you ever felt this way? Have you lost someone you really loved and do you miss them? God created us with a need for companionship. When we read the creation story, we see that everything God created was good. Then we get to Genesis 2:18 where it says, "It is not good for the man to be alone." God made us in his image and that means like him, we are relational social beings. We need other people in our lives. We have a natural longing to belong, to connect, to relate to other people.

There are all kinds of causes for loneliness. You may have relocated and don't know anyone in your area. You may have experienced the death of a loved one. You may live in a remote area and not have many neighbors or visitors. Perhaps you have devoted your life to your children, and now they've grown up and moved away and that's left a void in your life. You may have just become so busy with your career that you haven't devoted time to build relationships.

Whatever the reason, loneliness is something that no one wants to feel. Our inclination is to deny it, to run from it, and to avoid it at all costs. How do we do that? We start filling our lives with all kinds of stuff. It could be things like church activities, sports, TV, hobbies, or social networking. Yet, after our life is "full", we are still lonely. Why?

I think God has something else in mind for us when we are feeling lonely. I think we are supposed to accept it for what it is, and allow God to use it in our lives to make us depend on him. It's hard to admit we are lonely, because that makes us sound unpopular and needy. Yet denying the feelings won't make them go away.

Loneliness can cause us to reach out to others, perhaps people we would not have reached out to otherwise. It causes us to see others in a new way. When we are longing for someone to talk to, someone to care, someone to hug, we allow ourselves to reach out more. We may need to work on being friendly and approachable. One way to do this is to make eye contact with people and smile. Then, actively seek people out and start conversations. Some people do this naturally, I don't. Reaching out is difficult for me, and I have to purposefully make an effort to do so. I pray and ask God to help me to reach out to others.

In your loneliness, concentrate on hearing God's voice, that inner still small voice. If you allow it to, loneliness can actually lead you to a deeper relationship with God. When you have no one else to turn to, he is always there waiting for you. Don't fight your need to spend time with him. Face your loneliness and tell God about it. He already knows. He's just waiting for you to trust him with it. Take hold of his hand and walk with him. Allow him to comfort you and lift you up. Allow him to heal all the broken pieces. It sounds wrong but when you are lonely, spend some time alone with your Savior. Don't try to use busyness to cover your pain, it doesn't work.

I think Jesus understands our loneliness. Think about what life would have been like for him. He gave up his place in heaven to come and live a human life. He was the only sinless person here on earth. He had sinful parents and sinful siblings. Who did he have that could have been a "peer" for him? No one could really identify with what he was going through. His disciples didn't stand by him when he was arrested and later crucified. He went through the trial alone and then died alone. Think about what it must have been like for him when he died on the cross and when the Father turned his back on him. Jesus understood that by becoming sin for us, the Father could not have anything to do with him. He understands our loneliness.

After my best friend died, I had to really lean on the Lord. I had to tell him everything because there was no one else to talk to. There was no one else I could trust with my thoughts and my feelings. God used this pain in my life to continue to mature me. I also started to question some foundational things in my life; things like what am I spending my time doing? What is my real purpose? Am I doing all I am supposed to be doing for the Lord? Hard questions with no set answers.

If you are feeling lonely today, know that you are not alone. God has not forgotten you. He has promised that he will never leave you or forsake you (Hebrews 13:5). He loves you. He knows the very hairs on your head. He cares, and he understands. When everyone else fails you, Jesus will not. He is there waiting to take you by the hand and walk with you through your times of loneliness. Allow him to speak to you. Allow him to lead you. Allow him to challenge you in things you never dreamed you could do. God will help you through your lonely times, and he will provide the relationships you need. Just make sure you are truly putting him first, and remind yourself that as long as you have a close connection with God, you are never completely alone.

For further thought:

"Come near to God and he will come near to you." (James 4:8)

"For we do not have a high priest who is unable to empathize with our weaknesses, but we have one who has been tempted in every way, just as we are - yet he did not sin." (Hebrews 4:15)

"Let us then approach God's throne of grace with confidence, so that we may receive mercy and find grace to help us in our time of need." (Hebrews 4:16)

13 THE STORM OF APATHY (LUKEWARMNESS)

Unfortunately the following paragraph describes many Christians today. They have a nice marriage, nice children, a nice car (or 2), a nice house, and semi-regular church attendance. They go when it suits, but they are not all that serious. They don't want to seem radical about it. They put a little money in the offering plate, but it doesn't affect their budget or their standard of living. They aren't really concerned with sin in their lives as long as they aren't going to hell. They stand up and sit down at the right time. They sing, at least some of the words. They don't come to extra services. After all, they did their time on Sunday morning. They don't read their Bible through the week, or if they do, it is out of obligation not to hear from God. They don't talk about Jesus with anyone else. After all isn't their religion supposed to be private? They wouldn't want to offend anyone. Daily life is focused on their schedule, their to-do lists, their family, sports, etc. They don't ever really think about anything other than what's going on today. There's never any discussion about eternity. They do what they need to do to be "good enough." They look for the bare minimum in everything. Their life is so safe and structured, that they really don't need to trust God for anything. To sum it up, they accepted Christ at a young age, they were baptized, they came from a Christian family, and they go to church. What else is there?[1]

This is a sad depiction of the church today. We've lost the vision of what the Christian life is supposed to be like. We've lost our passion. We lack conviction, energy, and excitement in our faith. We are a textbook definition of "lukewarm" or "apathetic."

Revelation 3:15-16 was written to the church a Laodicea. "I know your deeds, that you are neither cold nor hot. I wish you were either one or the other! So, because you are lukewarm - neither hot nor cold - I am about to spit you out of my mouth."

Why was being lukewarm worse than being cold? Being lukewarm is being hypocritical. It is hypocritical to half-heartedly seek God. I think about what I see during worship times in our churches. No one seems excited. People are fidgeting. They are staring at their books. Some are singing but most are barely moving their mouths. The ones who are singing don't seem to have any joy in their singing. They don't seem to be paying attention to any of the words. People aren't connecting with God.

Worship is a time when we are to focus on God and who he is. He is our audience. We are singing to him. We are praising him.

Compare this scene with the stands at a ballgame. Everyone is focused on the next play. People are screaming and cheering. They are passionate about the events taking place. Now put those same people in a church pew on a Sunday morning, and they look like they are in agony. How that must grieve the heart of God! They are in the presence of the Creator of the universe, and they look completely disinterested, disconnected, bored.

Notice that this passage starts with "I know your deeds." What are my deeds? If someone were to look at my life and try to describe my Christian faith by what they see, what would they say? Jesus said, "This is to my Father's glory, that you bear much fruit, showing yourselves to be my disciples" (John 15:8). Jesus fully intended for me to be doing something with my faith. James says, "faith by itself, if it is not accompanied by action, is dead" (James 2:17).

So what am I doing? Am I bearing fruit? Am I loving my neighbor? If so, how? Am I reaching out to the lost, the lonely, the shut-ins, the widows? When is the last time I did something for someone else for no reason other than they needed some help? All of this needs to start in my heart. So how's my heart? And what am I doing to keep my heart in touch with God's heart?

Do I read my Bible daily? Do I pray? Or has my relationship with God become dry, routine, ritualistic, boring? What can I do to change that? Am I satisfied with being just godly enough to get into heaven? Do I compare my Christian life against other Christians and think, "well, at least I'm better than he is." Paul wrote, "Examine yourselves to see whether you are in the faith; test yourselves" (2 Corinthians 13:5). Am I a true follower of Christ or have I just been pretending? Have I really trusted him as my Savior? Being a Christian is more than just attending church, it's more than reciting a prayer, it's more than just good moral standards - it is a relationship with God. A Christian is someone in whom Christ dwells. And if the living Christ dwells in me, others will know it. There will be evidence of his presence in my life.

While my salvation is not earned by what I do, my works show that I have faith in Christ.

I've been this apathetic person at times in my life. It's easy to get sucked into it. I remember one specific time. We had joined a church with about 700 members. The church was growing and alive. The preaching was good. The kids' ministry time was good. The church just kept growing. When we got over 1500 on a Sunday morning, the church officials decided they needed to renovate the sanctuary. They knocked out all the classrooms to expand the main area. We had attended Sunday school, but they converted those classes into small groups that met throughout the week. That didn't work for us. A lot of new people were coming, and soon it seemed like we didn't know anyone. We started to get disconnected. Then we missed a couple of weeks, and no one even seemed to notice. Slowly we were pulling out of church, and I didn't even see it coming. Apathy can happen in very subtle ways. It could be something we do or don't do. It could be our attitudes. It could be the result of circumstances that just leave us feeling, "why should I even try anymore?"

So how do we overcome apathy? How do we get rid of being lukewarm? I'd like to suggest three things that come from Psalm 51.

The first is to *remember your conversion.* Do you remember what your life was like before you accepted Christ and how your life changed? Do you remember the excitement and the joy that salvation brought you? In Psalm 51:12, David asks the Lord to "restore to me the joy of your salvation." Pray and ask the Lord to remind you of just how great it is to be saved.

Next, recognize that *apathy (lukewarmness) is a sin* and repent of it. You've lost sight of God's plan for your life and his importance in your life. You've forgotten to love the Lord with all your heart, soul, and mind (Matthew 22:37). You've distanced yourself from God. In Psalm 51:2, David asks the Lord to cleanse him from his sin. Pray and admit to the Lord that you aren't loving him with your whole heart and ask him to help you do that.

Lastly, *ask the Lord to give you the strength and dedication to seek him every day.* You don't want to just know about the Lord, you want to love him, praise him, and serve him every day of your life. David asks the Lord in Psalm 51:10 to "renew a steadfast spirit within me." Ask the Holy Spirit to empower you to live a life pleasing to God.

We must realize that apathy, lukewarmness, laziness, indifference are the opposite of what God has called us to be. Satan, on the other hand, loves lukewarm apathetic Christians. Why? Because they are ineffective for the kingdom. We need to stay alert to this temptation. We must never forget that God is always with us. We need to worship and praise God, and let him control our lives each and every day. We must recognize that God is good, he's in control, and he has a purpose for us.

For further thought:

"The Lord says: 'These people come near to me with their mouth and honor me with their lips, but their hearts are far from me. Their worship of me is based on merely human rules they have been taught.' " (Isaiah 29:13)

"Never be lacking in zeal, but keep your spiritual fervor, serving the Lord." (Romans 12:11)

"Look to the LORD and his strength; seek his face always." (1 Chronicles 16:11)

"You will seek me and find me when you seek me with all your heart." (Jeremiah 29: 13)

14 THE STORM OF REJECTION

What exactly is rejection? It is the idea of not being good enough, not being accepted, or something that can't be used. Rejection can come in the form of a proposal being rejected, a college student not getting into a specific school, or it may be something as major as one spouse rejecting another or a parent rejecting a child. You may have experienced it in the form of a lost job. The degree of the rejection is irrelevant; rejection in any amount is always painful.

How did you respond? Did you feel like just giving up? Did you recoil and take cover, protecting yourself against additional pain? Did you throw a "pity party"? Did you withdraw from life and people? Did you feel like you were worthless? Did you feel like you weren't important or even necessary? Did you feel like nobody cared?

Relationships are messy, and when they start to fall apart the results can be devastating. Your sense of identity can get wrapped up in being a spouse, a parent, a child, a friend, an employee, etc.

When that relationship is threatened, so is your sense of self. Rejection destroys your self-esteem and attacks who you are. You feel like your life is being ripped apart at the core.

I've experienced all these feelings and few more. Rejection hurts deeply. The pain is intense, and it doesn't go away quickly. I felt like my life was a mess. I was hurt deeply. I didn't know what to do? Where was I to turn?

First and foremost, I went to Jesus. I understood that God never wants me to feel rejected or abandoned. His desire is for me to know who I am, and how deeply he loves me. I told him everything I was feeling and what my problems were. I trusted him to provide me with my self-worth. I trusted him to comfort me and to remind me of my true identity. I trusted him to uphold me, protect me, and guide me through this storm in my life. I completely surrendered everything in my life to him. I understood that God's approval is the only one that really mattered. I spent time reading my Bible and asking God to direct me to passages of scripture that would remind me who I am in Christ.

Whenever we base our identity on someone or something other than God's Word, we open ourselves up to rejection. As I worked through the process of rediscovering who I was, I wrote the following list and then I posted it on my computer monitor so I would see it every day.

In Christ, I am …
- Loved by the Father. (John 17:23)
- Forgiven of my sins. (1 John 1:9)
- Protected from the evil one. (John 17:15)
- Saved by faith. (Ephesians 2:8-9)

- Justified by faith. (Romans 5:1)
- Part of a royal priesthood. (1 Peter 2:9)
- An overcomer. (1 John 4:4)
- Reconciled to God. (2 Corinthians 5:18)
- Blessed with every spiritual blessing in the heavenly places. (Ephesians 1:3)
- Holy and blameless in God's sight. (Ephesians 1:4)
- Strengthened with power through his Spirit. (Ephesians 3:16)
- Not needy. (Philippians 4:19)
- Not fearful. (2 Timothy 1:7)
- Redeemed. (Galatians 3:13)
- Adopted into the family of God. (Ephesians 1:4-5)

As I read these each day, I was reminded of how God sees me. I was encouraged and strengthened in my faith. I was able to focus my mind on truth and not on the lies that Satan wanted to feed me. I started seeing myself for who I am in Christ; the person that God created me to be. Psalm 139 says that I was fearfully and wonderfully made. He knew me and everything about me before I was even born. He had plans for my life. Ephesians 2:10 says that I am God's handiwork and that I was created to do good works that God planned in advance for me. There is purpose and hope to life.

Rejection wounded my spirit, and those wounds were deep and painful. Spending time with God allowed him the opportunity to heal me. God alone can meet all my needs for acceptance and security. His desire for me was for me to start seeing myself for who I truly am. My identity must come from him and what his Word says about me. His Word will never change and God's love for me will never change. He will never turn his back on me, and nothing can destroy my position in Christ.

Moving forward, I asked God to help me consider the value of my current relationships. I prayed for wisdom to determine whether people in my life were worthy of my trust. I looked at who was influencing my life and whether their influences were positive or negative. I asked God to help me see what he wanted me to learn as a result of the pain I had experienced. I asked him to help me overcome my struggles with insecurity. I tried to understand the idea that rejection is more about the other person's inability to love than it is about my worthiness to be loved. Only God can love me perfectly, and I can count on him to do that 100% of the time. I asked God to help me let go of the past and move forward. Holding on to pain gets in the way of God's healing. I wanted to exchange the pain for joy. I was reminded of Psalm 51 where David asks God to restore to him the joy of his salvation. That's what I wanted – joy. That kind of joy only comes when we completely trust God with everything.

So how do you move past rejection? Pray, trust God with everything, and remember who you are – a child of the King!

For further thought:

"The righteous cry out, and the LORD hears them; he delivers them from all their troubles. The LORD is close to the brokenhearted and saves those who are crushed in spirit." (Psalm 34:17-18)

"What, then, shall we say in response to these things? If God is for us, who can be against us?" (Romans 8:31)

"All those the Father gives me will come to me, and whoever comes to me I will never drive away." (John 6:37)

"Take delight in the LORD, and he will give you the desires of your heart. Commit your way to the LORD; trust in him and he will do this: He will make your righteous reward shine like the dawn, your vindication like the noonday sun." Psalm 37:4-6

15 THE STORM OF STRESS

The dictionary defines stress as "mental, emotional, or physical strain or tension."[1] Stress seems to be at an all-time high in our culture today. Stress isn't something new. It's been around since the fall of man. People have a variety of ways of dealing with stress. Some cope through addictions to alcohol, over-eating, shopping, spending, etc. Addictions only provide temporary relief to stress. Eventually it takes more and more of the thing they are addicted to in order to satisfy them and that results in more frustration and stress.

I totally understand stress. There have been times when my life felt totally out of control. There was one point in my life when I was trying to balance the responsibilities of being a mom, a wife, a teacher, a coach, a student, and a daughter. I had so many identities that even I got confused. I had really stretched the limits of what one person could handle. I had too much to do and too many places I needed to be. I was stressed!

What causes stress? It usually boils down to one thing, not trusting God. We know that God is sovereign. We believe that he is able to take care of us. We know that he has given us everything that we need for life. So most of the time when we get stressed out, it is simply that we have forgotten to trust him. Our eyes are no longer on Jesus; they are on the chaos. We are trying to get things done in our own strength instead of allowing Christ to work in us and through us. The devil isn't stressing us out. Our spouse isn't stressing us out. Our boss isn't stressing us out. We've brought this on ourselves. I know you are thinking that I am way over simplifying this. The answer has to be more complex than that! If it were just as easy as trusting God, then how is my life this crazy?

What does the Bible say about stress? Jesus said, "Let not your hearts be troubled. Believe in God; believe also in me" (John 14:1). He is the only one who can give us the strength we need to cope with the troubles in our lives. Believing in him does not mean the troubles will magically vanish. It means that he will help us cope with the stress of life.

Paul had every reason to be stressed out. Five times Paul received 39 lashes from the Jews. Three times he was beaten with rods. He was stoned. Three times he was shipwrecked. He was constantly on the move. He was constantly in danger. And that's not to mention all the time he spent in jail. Yet in all of this, Paul never complained. We never read about him being tired, or hungry, or scared. He was confident that God would lead him and take care of him. He truly believed "to live is Christ, to die is gain" (Philippians 1:21). What did Paul do when he faced difficulties? He prayed, believed, rejoiced, and then rested.

I think Paul was able to see the big picture. Too often we focus on the small things in our lives. We magnify our troubles, and then they seem much larger than they really are. As they get blown out of proportion, we forget that Jesus loves us. We forget that he has promised to be with us through everything. We forget that we are to rely on God's strength and not on our own. We lose sight of the idea that God is at work through every circumstance and every situation – whether good or bad. We need to try to put everything back into its proper perspective. No matter what the stress is that is in our lives, God is still in control. This is the same God who spoke the universe into existence, he can handle anything and everything in our lives. We just need to allow him to handle it.

There are a few practical ideas for handling stress. When it comes to stress in our families, we need to realize that all families have stress. The amount of stress can vary depending on the size of our family and the age of our children. We need to try to see our families the way God does and enjoy our time with them. Children grow up quickly. Whatever stage we are in right now is temporary.

Some people experience stress in the work place. We need to try to find a job that we enjoy, because we are going to be spending a lot of time there. We need to get to know the people we work with, but try to stay out of the "drama." We need to remember that we are to represent Christ on the job, and that is hard to do if we get drawn into petty issues. And whatever we do, we need to let our work at the office. That stress doesn't need to come home with us.

Dealing with people can cause stress. While this can be at work, it can also be at the store, driving down the highway, or even at church. Remember that we are to show God's love to everyone around us. We are to let our light shine before men (people), and we are to live a life that is filled with peace and joy (Matthew 5:16; John 15:11), a life that others would envy. We are not to react impulsively, but to be patient with people with whom we come into contact. When that car cuts us off on the highway, or that person cuts line in the grocery store, or that sales clerk is short with us, we are to respond with patience and love. We don't really know what is going on in that other person's life.

God sees our stressful times as opportunities for us to grow in trust, strength, love, and perseverance. If we allow him to, he can use the stressful times in our lives to mature us in our faith and develop our Christian character. When stress comes our way, we need to recognize it, prioritize our lives (make sure God is first), pray, and then meet it head on.

For further thought:

"for everyone born of God overcomes the world. This is the victory that has overcome the world, even our faith." (1 John 5:4)

"I have told you these things, so that in me you may have peace. In this world you will have trouble. But take heart! I have overcome the world." (John 16:33)

"we are more than conquerors through him who loved us." (Romans 8:37)

16 THE STORM OF STRUGGLING IN PRAYER

I know some people who open their mouths and start praying and it all sounds so amazing and articulate. They leave me completely spellbound. How did they do that? How did they know what to say? How did they say it so well? I was sure God listened to them. However, sometimes I wondered if he heard me. I am shy and sometimes have a hard time communicating. I definitely feel this way when I try to pray in front of other people. I have so much on my heart I want to communicate, but it just doesn't come out.

That reminds me of a story. I was in a speech class in high school; I think it was ninth grade. I didn't want to take this class, but it was required. The day came for my first speech. I got up and took my notecards up to the podium in the front of the room. I put them down and had them arranged and ready to go. Then I walked over to the open door and walked out and down the hall. I had decided I couldn't do it, and so I simply walked out. The teacher came after me. He was very nice and talked me into coming back in the room and presenting my speech to the class. I don't remember what it was about or what grade I got. All I remember is that I was petrified to be in front of people.

Perhaps that is a story to which you can relate. Fear of public speaking is a common phobia. But there was more to my prayer struggles than just being afraid of people. I also struggled with what I was praying for. Do I pray for big things? Do I pray for specific things? Do I really believe God is going to answer? Do I truly believe he can do the things I am praying about?

I believe God can do anything, and that he desires to show us he loves us. I believe that he can and does do miracles. Probably many more than he ever gets credit for. And if I truly believe these things, then my prayer life should reflect those beliefs. I should pray for big things, the kind of things that are supernatural. I need to trust and not worry about how he answers my prayers. Answers are his business not mine. I need to pray and believe and not be afraid of being disappointed. Too many times my prayers have such low expectations that it would be hard to even see if God answered them. I have not, because I ask not (James 1:6; Matthew 7:7).

Asking in faith brings glory to God. When I come to him and ask, I am recognizing my need for him and my dependence on him. He is glorified by my obedience in asking and by my belief in asking. None of that has anything to do with how he chooses to answer my prayer. Actually, my hope is in God, not in a specific answer to prayer. God is perfectly wise, always good, and always right. My hope stands firm on those facts along with the fact that God never changes. He is the same yesterday, today, and forever

(Hebrews 13:8). I am confident that whatever he chooses to do will flow from his perfect wisdom and his boundless love for me.

God is in the miracle business. I can't read the Bible and not see the examples of God displaying his power and his glory through the working of miracles. And since he doesn't change, there is no reason to question his ability to continue to perform miracles today. I can be sure of one thing: if I don't ask, he won't answer. I need to never be afraid to ask. So what stops me? Why don't I pray for big things?

The sin of unbelief keeps me from experiencing the supernatural works of God in my life. It paralyzes me. The Bible tells us that without faith, it is impossible to please God (Hebrews 11:6). Nothing reveals what I really want and what I really think about God more than my prayers. My prayers reveal whether I want God's will or my own. My prayers reveal what I think about God, how much I trust him, and how much faith I truly have. My hesitancy to pray for big things reveals a problem with my heart, not a problem with my God.

I believe God is alive and well and longing to give good gifts to his children. I think he wants to display his power and his glory through miraculous works, if we would only pray for them, and then believe they will happen. And even if he chooses not to answer the way I am asking, that's OK. That doesn't change who he is or my faith in him.

Do you remember the story of Shadrach, Meshach, and Abednego from Daniel 3? They were about to be tossed into the fiery furnace for not worshipping the king's idol. They expressed unwavering confidence in the ability of God to save them. They weren't confident God *would* save them but they were confident that he *could*. They believed there was something worse than dying because God chose not to save them. What could be worse – serving a god who couldn't deliver them if he wanted to. And that was precisely what King Nebuchadnezzar was requiring them to do. So they chose to remain faithful to God, even though they were going to be put to death. What happened next is amazing! After they were thrown into the furnace, the king saw four men in the furnace, not three, and the fourth looked "like a son of the gods" (Daniel 3:25). Who joined them in furnace? Jesus! He chose not to stop them from being tossed into the fiery ordeal, but to be right beside them through every step of the way. They were then released from the furnace and were completely unharmed. Sometimes when we pray for God to take away a trial, his choice is to let us go through it, but he is beside us every step of the way.

My job is to pray and then move forward in faith, believing God and his Word and be thankful. Going back to my story in the beginning of this chapter, I need to remember that it isn't the flowery words that I speak that moves the heart of God. Some people say all the right things, but their hearts just aren't in it. It is more important that I talk to God out of a humble repentant heart and really be honest before God about what my needs are. I need to hang in there with God in prayer and not run out the door when things are uncomfortable. God is able to do abundantly beyond what I can ask, or think, or imagine (Ephesians 3:20). So pray the big prayers, believe in miracles, and sit back and watch God work.

For further thought:

"Ask and it will be given to you; seek and you will find; knock and the door will be opened to you." (Matthew 7:7)

"But when you ask, you must believe and not doubt, because the one who doubts is like a wave of the sea, blown and tossed by the wind." (James 1:6)

"And he could do no miracle there except that he laid his hands on a few sick people and healed them. And he wondered at their unbelief." (Mark 6:5-6)

17 THE STORM OF TEMPTATION

One of the challenges of being a Christian is how we deal with temptation on a daily basis. Temptations come in the most interesting and wonderful packages. If they didn't look good, we wouldn't be tempted. Each of us is tempted differently. Things that tempt me might not tempt you. Don't be surprised by temptation, in fact, be on guard and expect it. Then when it appears, deal with it quickly and correctly.

I recently heard the statement, "sometimes all you can do is the next *right thing*." That statement stuck with me and I really gave it some thought. As a Christian this is the only response we should ever have. No matter what the world thinks or does, we should do the *right thing*. That *right thing* might not seem normal to the world. If we are at work and everyone else is "cheating" the company, we need to do the *right thing*. When everyone else is taking long lunches, we need to do the *right thing*. When others are simply not doing their job, we need to do the *right thing*. When others lie on their time cards, we need to do the *right thing*. When others are cheating on their spouses, we need to do the *right thing*. The acceptable thing and the *right thing* are often in opposition to each other. We must not worry about anyone else; simply focus on our own responsibilities and do what we need to do.

I've heard this statement my whole life, "If you don't stand for something, you'll fall for anything." This is a powerful statement that drives home the point of having convictions, and the integrity and strength of character to stick by them and stand up for them. We never know who is watching, and who our right actions can influence. The Bible talks about choosing whom we are going to serve (Joshua 24:15). It also talks about us being salt and light to the world (Matthew 5). Step out of your comfort zone and determine what the *right thing* is to do, and then just do it. Don't worry about what anyone else will think.

Matthew 4 tells the story about Jesus being tempted. Verse 3 says, "The tempter came to him and said, "If you are the Son of God, tell these stones to become bread." What's the big deal? Jesus was hungry. He had just fasted for 40 days. He had the power to turn stones into bread. He could do something about his hunger. He could satisfy his need himself. That was his temptation. There is nothing wrong with eating. Everyone has to have food to live, so Satan whispered to Jesus, "Why not go ahead and change the stones into loaves of bread?" Jesus knew this was not the right thing to do. Jesus knew the devil was tempting him to fulfill his need for food in his own way, by his own plan, rather than waiting for God's perfect timing. Satan was tempting Jesus to use his power for selfish purposes.

Did you ever wonder what it would be like to be Jesus? You are fully human, and yet you have God's power. You could walk on water anytime you wanted. If someone makes fun of you, you could make his own hand slap him. You could fly into work on the wings of the angels. Yet Jesus never used his power for himself. He only used it to benefit others. He healed the sick, caused the lame to walk, made the blind to see, and raised the dead.

This is a great lesson for us to learn. Satan would have us believe that the things with which he tempts us are for our own good. Sadly, many of us believe that lie. What we really need to do is look beyond the immediate benefits of the current temptation and see the situation for what it really is. We need to get the big picture from God's perspective. We need to see the long term effects of our decisions, and we need to be sure we are making the right decision.

How did Jesus respond to the devil? Jesus answered, "It is written: 'Man shall not live on bread alone, but on every word that comes from the mouth of God' " (Matthew 4:4).

Jesus' response to Satan was to quote scripture. Jesus was telling Satan that there are other things in life much more important than bread - bread gives strength to our body, but that will eventually die, anyway. However, the Word of God gives strength to the soul and that will live forever.

Paul writes the following in 1 Corinthians:

> No temptation has overtaken you except what is common to mankind. And God is faithful; he will not let you be tempted beyond what you can bear. But when you are tempted, he will also provide a way out so that you can endure it. (1 Corinthians 10:13)

God promises us that he will never let Satan go too far. With God's help, we will be able to endure temptation, and we will be able to escape it. However, we need to know God's Word so we can recognize the temptation for what it is, and use the escape that is available. As Christians, we can find power and wisdom in the Word of God, we can rely on God's strength and power in times of temptation, and we can do "the next right thing."

For further thought:

"Thy word have I hid in mine heart, that I might not sin against thee." (Psalm 10:13)

"When tempted, no one should say, 'God is tempting me.' For God cannot be tempted by evil, nor does he tempt anyone." (James 1:13)

"You are the salt of the earth. But if the salt loses its saltiness, how can it be made salty again? It is no longer good for anything, except to be thrown out and trampled by men. 'You are the light of the world. A city on a hill cannot be hidden. Neither do people light a lamp and put it under a bowl. Instead they put it on its stand, and it gives light to everyone in the house. In the same way, let your light shine before men, that they may see your good deeds and praise your Father in heaven.' " (Matthew 5:13-16)

18 THE STORM OF WEARINESS

Life is hard. Perhaps life has pushed you physically and emotionally to the point where you are just weary and worn out. The battle that we call life can sometimes seem like an uphill fight. We are tired and we want to give up, and yet there is hope. Jesus said, "Come to me, all you who are weary and burdened, and I will give you rest" (Matthew 11:28).

Weariness is not what God wants for us. What Jesus said was that he would provide the rest that we needed when we come to him with all of the stuff that is making us weary. God never grows weary. He never gets tired and he never needs to rest.

> Do you not know? Have you not heard? The LORD is the everlasting God, the Creator of the ends of the earth. He will not grow tired or weary, and his understanding no one can fathom. (Isaiah 40:28)

In our culture today, many people live from one vacation to the next. They will just get home from one vacation, and they start planning the next one. Personally, I start counting the days until the next break from school. It's not that I will go anywhere special or do anything extraordinary, it's just the break from work that I look forward to having. We all love to relax and rest.

We shouldn't forget God's original plan. We were to take one day of rest for every six days that we work. God planned it that way because he knew we needed to rest each week. Jesus confirmed the need for the Sabbath in Mark 2:27. I have found when I obey the principle of taking a Sabbath day each week; I am less likely to grow weary. Each person has to figure out what that means for him. A day of rest for me means after church, I get to read a book, watch a video, or take a nap. You know - something that is enjoyable and does not require me to exert mental, physical, or emotional energy. I have had times when I even included abstaining from computer activities on Sundays, because once I get on the computer, I seem to get drawn into working.

As I am thinking about weariness, I am reminded of one of my favorite passages of scripture.

> And let us run with perseverance the race marked out for us, fixing our eyes on Jesus, the pioneer and perfecter of faith. For the joy set before him he endured the cross, scorning its shame, and sat down at the right hand of the throne of God. Consider him who endured such opposition from sinners, so that you will not grow weary and lose heart. (Hebrews 12:1-3)

The race that the writer of Hebrews is referring to is a marathon not a sprint. We are called to stay the course and remain faithful to the end. Paul talked about this in 2 Timothy 4:7 where he said, "I have fought the good fight, I have finished the race, I have kept the faith."

My husband has run two marathons. He will tell you that it is a test of endurance. You train for a long time, but you never really understand the race until you are in it. It requires faith, stamina, commitment, and discipline in order to finish. You will get to places in the race where you think you just can't go on any more, then you dig a little deeper and keep going. Unlike the marathons that my husband ran, each Christian has his own unique marathon.

God establishes our course and our finish line. We need to stay on the course, no matter what obstacles we encounter. I can't run your race for you, and you can't run mine for me. We aren't in competition with each other, we are on the same team. As we each run our own race, we need to be encouraging one another to finish strong. There will be times when the finish line seems to be a long way away, and we will be tempted to quit. It is during these times that we need to choose to put our faith in Christ and keep going.

We need to pray for strength and endurance. We are to focus our eyes on Jesus and examine the way he ran the race. His race was filled with hatred, bitterness, and opposition and yet he finished it flawlessly. He never faltered. He never lost sight of the goal.

Don't look at the distractions, don't look at the other runners, and don't look at your circumstances. All of those things will cause you to grow weary.

Growing weary is easy. Our natural tendency when things get tough is to lose heart and want to give up. We start to think that our race is impossible and wonder why God allowed all these obstacles on our course. We look at someone else's course, and we wonder why they got an easy course, and we got difficult ones. We have a hard time even seeing the finish line. And then just when it seems like things can't get any worse, we look up and who do we see? Jesus! He's running next to us and helping us avoid the obstacles and make it to our finish line. The writer of Hebrews tells us to consider what Jesus endured. When we do that, we start to realize that our lives aren't so bad after all. I am the first to admit that life is sometimes hard and fighting battles everyday can make me weary. So how do we overcome weariness? We fix our eyes on Jesus.

The writer goes on to say that Jesus endured the cross because of the joy that was set before him. In other words, he was focused on what was to come next – after the cross.

Keep your focus on Jesus and your eyes on your destination. Don't let things that come up along the way discourage you or get you off track. Keep your relationship with God strong. Spending time with him will help refresh you when you are weary. Find other people you can talk to about your faith. Be a support system for each other. Hebrews 10:24 says we should "consider how we may spur one another on toward love and good deeds." Paul says in 1 Thessalonians 5:11 that we should "encourage one another and build each other up." So run your race with perseverance, focus on Jesus, and I'll see you at the finish line.

For further thought:

"but those who hope in the LORD will renew their strength. They will soar on wings like eagles; they will run and not grow weary, they will walk and not be faint." (Isaiah 40:31)

"Let us not become weary in doing good, for at the proper time we will reap a harvest if we do not give up." (Galatians 6:9)

"never tire of doing what is good." (2 Thessalonians 3:13)

19 THE STORM OF ANGER

Sometimes things happen in life that make us angry. Anger itself is not a sin. No one should expect us to act like everything is good when it isn't. Somewhere along the way, we've gotten the idea that a good Christian has it together all the time and we never get angry. God created us with a range of emotions, and anger is one of them. Being angry is not the issue, the issue is whether we allow anger to control us.

James tells us that we are to be "slow to anger" (James 1:19). Controlling our tempers and our anger demonstrates strength and maturity. No one wants to be around a "hot head" who flies off the handle at the slightest inconvenience. However, too many times we go to the other extreme, and we put on our good Christian face. We stuff our anger, and we let it control us. We hold a grudge because we aren't willing to deal with it. This kind of anger can tear relationships apart.

Probably one of the most well-known stories in the Bible when talking about anger is when Jesus drove the money-changers from the temple. The merchants were selling animals for sacrifices at an inflated rate. They were robbing people who came to exchange currency to buy animals. They had made a mockery of God's temple. So, Jesus made a whip, and physically drove them out of the temple. He overturned their tables (John 2:13-18). He was angry that the people had defiled God's house. When nobody else seemed to care, Jesus took action and did something about the problem. This was righteous anger. This was anger at sin.

So why do we get angry? Anger can stem from injustices we see in the world, impatience, jealousy, abuse of any kind, or unmet needs. Anger can come from a losing job or contracting a serious illness. Anger can also arise from being cheated on or lied to. Anger is a natural response to being hurt. The pain from the loss of a loved one can cause anger. This list could go on and on.

So what do you do when you get angry? First, choose to calm down. Have you ever been told to count to 10 before reacting? This is actually a great idea. It may keep you from saying something you will regret later. It will give you time to think through your response and if you even want to respond at all. Think about whether it is even worth getting angry about the situation. Many times if you think it through, you will realize that it just isn't worth the time or emotional energy that it requires. Try to figure out exactly what caused the anger; was it a person or a situation? Get to the root cause of the problem. Be willing to surrender your anger to the Lord, and seek his purposes in the situation.

Sometimes when we are angry, the person who angered us isn't even aware of it. We need to choose how we are going to handle our anger. I've been through some rough times in my life, and some of those caused me to be angry. I had a choice to make.

Allow the Holy Spirit to control my life or allow my sinful nature to control my life. I could turn to the Lord for patience and strength, or I could allow my anger to run unchecked. Proverbs 14:17 says, "A quick-tempered person does foolish things."

Another thing I needed to consider was the idea that God didn't want me to become a "doormat." I needed to protect myself from being hurt, without sinking to the same level as the person who was hurting me. Angry outbursts solve nothing. I need to remember that once words are spoken, I can't take them back. Even if I apologize later, the damage has been done. And while an angry outburst may make me feel better for a few minutes, it doesn't solve the problem that caused the anger. An angry outburst will also ruin my Christian testimony. How will that other person take my faith seriously if I can't even control my anger?

Jesus promised us troubles in this world. He also told us to be shrewd as snakes and as innocent as doves (Matthew 10:16). The truth is that stinky stuff happens to us all the time. If we are both shrewd and innocent, we will be prepared to meet the problems head on and deal with them in a manner that would honor God.

Anger can become sin when it is coupled with pride, when it is allowed to linger, or when it serves no purpose. One thing to think about is am I directing my anger at a problem, or am I directing it at a person. The Bible specifically tells us that we are to use our words to build each other up. We are to speak the truth in love – not in anger (Ephesians 4:15). We are to leave room for God's wrath and not seek vengeance (Romans 12:19). God is righteous and just. He will handle the offense against us with perfect justice.

Surrender your anger to God, and let him deal with the situation for you. If we read farther into Romans 12, we see that verse 21 tells us to repay evil with good. This can only be done by choosing to do it. You won't feel like doing it. It's not a natural thing for someone to do, but it is what God tells us to do. Finally, base every decision you make on scripture. Start committing scripture to memory. Then when you are in the midst of a bad situation, pray that the Holy Spirit will direct you.

Anger is inescapable. Where you need to be careful is how you express it and how you manage it. Are you angry at sin or is your anger sin? Ephesians 4:26 says, "In your anger do not sin." Think carefully about how you will respond and ask the Lord to guide your response. Do what Paul suggests, be kind, compassionate, and forgiving to those who made you angry (Ephesian 4:32). Why? Because Jesus has already been kind, compassionate, and forgiving to you.

For further thought:

"My dear brothers and sisters, take note of this: Everyone should be quick to listen, slow to speak and slow to become angry, because human anger does not produce the righteousness that God desires." (James 1:19-20)

"Whoever is patient has great understanding, but one who is quick-tempered displays folly." (Proverbs 14:29)

" 'In your anger do not sin': Do not let the sun go down while you are still angry, and do not give the devil a foothold." (Ephesians 4:26-27)

"Do not let any unwholesome talk come out of your mouths, but only what is helpful for building others up according to their needs, that it may benefit those who listen. And do not grieve the Holy Spirit of God, with whom you were sealed for the day of redemption. Get rid of all bitterness, rage and anger, brawling and slander, along with every form of malice. Be kind and compassionate to one another, forgiving each other, just as in Christ God forgave you." (Ephesians 4: 29-32)

20 THE STORM OF LIES (DECEIT)

Trust is foundational in all relationships. When we trust someone and begin to share our life with that person, we do so because we trust him. We believe he says what he means and means what he says. Lying is defined as "making a false statement with the intent to deceive."[1]

The Bible makes it clear that lying is a sin. The Ten Commandments include, "You shall not bear false witness against your neighbor" (Exodus 20:16). Acts 5 tells the story of Ananias and Sapphira and how they lied about a donation they were making to the church. Verse 3 says, "Ananias, how is it that Satan has so filled your heart that you have lied to the Holy Spirit and have kept for yourself some of the money you received for the land?" God found this lie so offensive that it cost this couple their lives.

Jesus said he is the way, the truth, and the life (John 14:6). If Jesus is truth, then it follows that his people should tell the truth. Hebrews 6:18 says it is impossible for God to lie. Our actions are a reflection of our character and our faith. Being honest is not always easy, but it is always right. We need to work at being truthful in all things.

Why do we lie? Fear is one reason why we don't tell the truth. We are afraid of the consequences if we tell the truth. This really means we don't trust God to take care of the situation. Pride is another reason why we lie. We are concerned about what people will think of us. We desire man's approval over obeying God. Sometimes we lie, because we have something to hide. We have a secret we don't want you to know. When we lie, we are showing that we do not care about your feelings. We might lie because it seems like the easy way out. We don't think we will get caught. Once we start lying, the next lie is a little easier, and the next one a little easier. Pretty soon we have no idea what the truth is.

Is there ever a time when lying is the right thing to do? What about "white lies"? A white lie is usually one that is considered unimportant. It could be that you are trying to be polite or trying to "keep the peace" in a relationship. Common white lies include lying about your age, lying about your weight, lying about your golf score, or even lying about the fish that got away. In many ways, these lies seem acceptable because no one got hurt.

However, I don't think God views them that way. Proverbs 6:17 says that God detests a lying tongue and it doesn't give any exceptions to that rule. When we lie, even a white lie, it ruins our integrity. White lies are usually told because they are easy for us – in other words, they are selfish. Ephesians 4:15 says we are to speak the truth in love. Sometimes telling the truth isn't easy, but it is always the right thing to do. Being truthful honors the Lord.

So what are some other common ways that Christians get enticed into lying? Did you ever tell someone you were going to do something and then not do it? Do you cheat on your income taxes? Did you ever have your spouse tell someone that you weren't home when you were? Did you ever compliment someone and not really mean it? Did you ever exaggerate the truth? Did you ever say, "I'll call you tomorrow," and not really mean it? Did you ever say, "I would be happy to do that for you," and not mean it?

I was thinking about the seriousness of telling someone else that I would pray for him/her. When people have told you that they would pray for you, have you ever wondered if they really did? The Pew Research Center did a poll in late 2012 that showed that only 3% of people who said, "I will pray for you," actually said a prayer. People gave a variety of reasons for not following through, including: "I forgot, I already had too many things to pray for, I didn't actually mean it, and it's just a figure of speech."[2]

We should never take prayer lightly. God hears all our prayers. When we tell someone we will pray for them, that's like making a promise. What can we do to help keep our verbal commitment to pray? I think the best way is to go ahead and pray for that person immediately. Whatever we are doing, stop, take a minute, and pray for that person or situation.

That reminds me of when my mom was in the hospital to have surgery for uterine cancer. A pastor came in to see her. He was doing rounds and visiting people who were in the hospital. We didn't know this man, but as we talked, we learned that we had a pastor friend in common. We found it easy to talk about our friend. As this man was turning to leave, he told my mom that he would pray for her. The idea that he was just going to talk to her and leave, shocked me. I didn't understand why he didn't pray with her while he was there. We obviously weren't going to object. We had just talked about our church and had indicated that we were Christians. But he didn't pray with her, he just left with a promise to pray. I wondered if he really meant it. I wondered if he carried through on his promise to pray.

No one likes being lied to. It's a horrible feeling to know we have been deceived, that someone we trusted, lied to us. As Christians we need to ask the Lord if we are guilty of lying or deceit. We want to keep our word so that people will know that we are honest and trustworthy. If we are known to lie about some things then how can anyone trust anything we have to say? How will they know that when we are talking about Jesus we are telling the truth. Why would they want to listen to people who are known for not telling the truth.

God always keeps his word. He is faithful to every promise he has made. Because he is reliable, we can trust him. We need to make it our aim to please him (2 Corinthians 5:9) and to live a life worthy of the gospel (Philippians 1:27). And that includes telling the truth, to everyone, all the time.

For further thought:

"God is not human, that he should lie, not a human being, that he should change his mind. Does he speak and then not act? Does he promise and not fulfill?" (Numbers 23:19)

"There are six things the LORD hates, seven that are detestable to him: haughty eyes, a lying tongue, hands that shed innocent blood, a heart that devises wicked schemes, feet that are quick to rush into evil, a false witness who pours out lies and a person who stirs up conflict in the community." (Proverbs 6:16-19)

"A false witness will not go unpunished, and whoever pours out lies will perish.' (Proverbs 19:9)

"Let us hold unswervingly to the hope we profess, for he who promised is faithful." (Hebrews 10:23)

21 THE STORM OF DISCONTENTMENT

Did you ever find yourself thinking things like: I wish I worked somewhere else. I wish I had a different boss. I wish I had different co-workers. I wish I had more money. I wish my husband/wife only understood me better, etc. This is what I call the "I wish" syndrome. Somehow you think life would be infinitely better if you could change some part of it.

I started thinking things like this recently. This is a trap that Satan uses to defeat Christians. It causes us to focus on things that either can't happen or aren't currently happening. It wastes our time and makes us inefficient. It makes us discontented with where the Lord has us today. Our focus is on ourselves, and not on the Lord.

Paul says in Philippians 4:11 that he has learned to be content in all circumstances. Contentment is not a natural thing, but something you have to learn. Wherever you are in life, take some time and look around you. Do you have anything for which you can stop and give thanks? In verse 4 of this same chapter, Paul writes, "Rejoice in the Lord always." No matter what is going on in your life, God knows about it. Nothing ever takes him by surprise. He never wonders what is going to happen next. He never questions anything or learns anything new.

We are abundantly blessed and have everything a person could possibly need, and yet we are bored and frustrated. Why – because things don't bring happiness or contentment. Contentment comes from a life that is yielded to Christ. It comes when we come to realize that what God offers us is far better than anything the world has to offer.

To be content means to be satisfied with what I am and what I have. God knows who I am. He knows everything there is to know about me. He has plans for my life. Ephesians 2:10 says that I was created in Christ to do good works that God prepared in advance for me to do. Sometimes I have trouble seeing his plan. This is especially true when I am in the middle of difficult circumstances. I have had many occasions in my life when I wondered why God would allow certain things to happen to me. There were so many things that I just didn't understand.

Discontentment can kill our spiritual growth. When we are discontented, it is like telling God that he isn't doing a good job. He isn't providing what I need.

The people of Israel were discontented with God. Do you remember how they complained to Moses? God had totally devastated Egypt with the plagues. He humiliated Pharaoh. He brought the Israelites safely through the Red Sea and destroyed the Egyptian army who was chasing them. The Israelites rejoiced, feared God, and put their trust in him (Exodus 14). But how long did that last? About as long as it took for them to run out of food and water. Then they grumbled and complained and actually wished they were back in slavery in Egypt. They quickly forgot their bondage, and all they could remember was they had food to eat. They completely lost perspective. They accused Moses and Aaron of bringing them out into the desert to die (Exodus 16). The Israelites didn't like the way God was handling things. Whenever they came to something that required that they have a little faith, they complained. They doubted God's goodness and his power. They were never able to rest and trust.

Are we any different? How do we react to difficulties? Do we get angry with God and wonder why he let things happen to us? Do we withdraw from God and refuse to talk to him? Do we recognize that God has provided for us and cared for us this far, and trust that he will continue to do that? Are we content to leave our situations in God's hands and allow him time to work things out? Do we really understand that God is in control and that he loves us? When we are in the middle of a bad situation, are we thinking about the "good old days," or are we embracing the day for what it is, and trusting that God will see us through? Discontentment steals our joy. We can't have joy and be grumbling at the same time.

In Philippians 4, Paul wrote that I can do all things through Christ who gives me strength. He also wrote that God will meet all my needs. It really comes down to whether I trust him or not. It's really all about choices: choosing to rejoice, choosing to pray about everything, choosing to believe God, choosing to be content, and choosing to trust. As I make these kinds of choices, I am able to replace the "I wishes" with: I am satisfied. I am content. I am trusting God.

For further thought:

"But godliness with contentment is great gain. For we brought nothing into the world, and we can take nothing out of it. But if we have food and clothing, we will be content with that. Those who want to get rich fall into temptation and a trap and into many foolish and harmful desires that plunge people into ruin and destruction. For the love of money is a root of all kinds of evil. Some people, eager for money, have wandered from the faith and pierced themselves with many griefs." (1 Timothy 6:6-10)

"Do everything without grumbling or arguing, so that you may become blameless and pure, 'children of God without fault in a warped and crooked generation.' " (Philippians 2:14-15)

"You will keep in perfect peace those whose minds are steadfast, because they trust in you." (Isaiah 26:3)

"Therefore I tell you, do not worry about your life, what you will eat or drink; or about your body, what you will wear. Is not life more than food, and the body more than clothes? Look at the birds of the air; they do not sow or reap or store away in barns, and yet your heavenly Father feeds them. Are you not much more valuable than they? Can any one of you by worrying add a single hour to your life?" (Matthew 6:25-27)

22 THE STORM OF GUILT

Many years ago I did something that was so stupid that looking back on it I wonder what in the world I was thinking. It was a Friday afternoon and I was in a meeting with my boss. He asked me a question, one that caught me completely off-guard. I hadn't done anything wrong, but I knew that if I told him the truth, it would look bad, even though it wasn't. So in a split second I made a horrible mistake. I lied. I heard myself saying things that I knew weren't true. It was almost like I was watching this scene unfold before me, and I wasn't a part of it. As I sat there, I couldn't believe my own ears. The meeting ended, and I walked out in disbelief. What had I just done? The weekend went by, and I felt so guilty I could hardly stand it. Monday morning I was back in his office, confessing to him what I had done and telling him the truth. He forgave me, but I still couldn't forgive myself. I got so focused on the wrong and wrapped up in the guilt and frustration that I temporarily lost sight of God. The guilt so blinded me that it kept me dwelling on my stupidity, and not on God's love and forgiveness. I struggled for a long time with forgiving myself. Lying was definitely not a part of my character. It wasn't who I was. How could I have been that stupid?

There's a difference between condemnation and conviction. I had just experienced both. Conviction comes from God, and its goal was to lead me to repentance. God had revealed this particular sin in my life, so that I could confess it and deal with it. His goal for me was to cleanse me, change my heart, and restore my relationship with him. Until I was willing to confess my sin to God and ask for forgiveness, my relationship with God was going to be broken.

God always convicts us of sin out of his love for us, and not in an effort to make us feel guilty or rejected. He knows everything we've done and he loves us anyway. He wants us to confess our sin so that he can show us his forgiveness and love. He wants to restore our relationship.

We all mess up and make mistakes. Romans 3:23 says, "all have sinned and fallen short of the glory of God." I've never met anyone who could honestly say that he had never sinned. If there are unconfessed sins in our lives, then a feeling of guilt can come from God. This is the Holy Spirit convicting our hearts and trying to get us to rectify our relationship with God. 1 John 1:9 says "If we confess our sins, he is faithful and just and will forgive us our sins and purify us from all unrighteousness." How do we do that? We simply tell God what we've done that was wrong, ask him to forgive us, and ask him to help us not to repeat that same mistake.

Remember that God's goal is never to bring guilt or condemnation to us by reminding us of our past sins. God wants to bring healing and restoration. Isaiah 43:25 says that God blots out our sins and remembers them no more. His desire is for us to see his grace and love. He leads us forward in our lives. He wants us to put the past behind us.

Sometimes even after we've confessed the sin to God and know that he has forgiven us, the guilty feelings remain. Guilt is one of Satan's biggest weapons. It tears us down and makes us feel useless. It robs us of our peace and joy. It keeps us from being who God created us to be. In Revelation 12:10, Satan is called the accuser of the brethren. He relentlessly reminds us of our failures, faults, and sins in an effort to cause us guilt and shame. He tries to use these to deceive us and keep us from trusting God.

Satan's voice brings hopelessness. He offers no way out. When the Holy Spirit brings conviction, he also brings with it hope, and an offer of freedom and blessing. The Holy Spirit brings us a desire for holiness and purity. While Satan's condemnation points out our problems only to judge us and make us feel guilty, God's conviction offers us a remedy for the problem and a way forward. God speaks to us out of love for us.

There is a story in John 8 that illustrates this point pretty well. It's a familiar story. A group of Pharisees have caught a woman in the act of adultery. They drag her into the temple area where Jesus is teaching. Their goal is two-fold: first, to publically expose and disgrace her and, second, to try to trap Jesus. Think about how the woman must have felt. The Pharisees had no desire to help her overcome her sin. They didn't care about her at all. They were just using her to try to discredit Jesus. Satan does the same thing today. His goal is to expose us, disgrace us, and discredit Jesus in the process.

The Pharisees were demanding that the Law of Moses be upheld which stated that the woman should be stoned. Then they made their mistake; they asked Jesus for his opinion. Jesus replied that if anyone was without sin, he was to throw the first stone. One by one they all dropped their rocks and walked away. Then Jesus, the only one qualified to throw a stone, told her that he didn't condemn her. He had chosen to show her forgiveness and grace. He didn't ignore her sin, he told her to change her life, but he didn't condemn her or make her feel guilty.

So if you feel like stones are being thrown at you, realize that Jesus doesn't throw stones. He convicts, but he doesn't condemn. He offers you love and grace and the opportunity to leave your life of sin behind you and move forward in righteousness. If guilty feelings remain, examine your heart. Ask yourself if you have repented of all your sin. If you have sincerely confessed your sin and repented, (turned away from it) then stand on the promises of 1 John 1:9 – that God has forgiven and cleansed you and that there is no longer any reason to feel guilty.

We can't change our past, but we can learn from it. One of the lessons we need to learn is to trust in, and meditate on, God's truth. We need to know what the Word says about how God sees us.

Remember that when we came to Christ we were made new creatures in him. 2 Corinthians 5:7 tells us that "the old has gone, the new has come." The old that is gone includes all our past sins and the guilt that they produce. Never look back on what you were, but look to who you are in Christ and what he has promised you in the future.

For further thought:

"Therefore, there is now no condemnation for those who are in Christ Jesus." (Romans 8:1)

"For God did not send his Son into the world to condemn the world, but to save the world through him. Whoever believes in him is not condemned, but whoever does not believe stands condemned already because they have not believed in the name of God's one and only Son." (John 3:17-18)

"When you were dead in your sins and in the uncircumcision of your flesh, God made you alive with Christ. He forgave us all our sins, having canceled the charge of our legal indebtedness, which stood against us and condemned us; he has taken it away, nailing it to the cross." (Colossians 2:13-14)

23 THE STORM OF PERFECTIONISM

Work harder. Achieve more. Do better. Don't make mistakes. Perfectionism is something that haunts many people. It can't be achieved, and yet many Christians continue to work towards this unattainable goal. They strive in their strength to do something that only God could do. They set their expectations for themselves so high that there's no way they can obtain those goals. Nothing is ever good enough. They don't see the positive or the good in anything; they can only see that it isn't quite perfect yet.

There's nothing wrong with working hard, and there's nothing wrong with doing a good job. The Bible tells us to do our work as unto the Lord (Colossians 3:23). We are supposed to be an example to the world around us. God loves it when we use the gifts and talents he has given us, whether teaching, cooking, operating machinery, or running a business. Working hard is not a bad thing, and many good things can come from our hard work.

However, many times society today places expectations on us that aren't healthy or godly. Mistakes aren't tolerated. Employees are cut down in front of others. Missing the goal is considered a failure, even if the goal is unrealistic. All of this translates into frustration, a loss in confidence, and burnout.

How does that translate into the Christian life? A Christian who is a perfectionist will try hard to be the best they can be for God. They will attend every service, Bible study, and prayer group. They will look at their spiritual life for ways to improve it, because there must be something else they can do. They couldn't possibly be doing all that God desires for them to do. As they become obsessed over things, they are becoming the opposite of what God wants for them in many ways.

The message of the gospel is that we need a Savior because we can't save ourselves. There's nothing we can do to earn our salvation. There's nothing that we can add to what Jesus has done for us. When we trust in him, he forgives our imperfections.

The Pharisees were a good example of perfectionists. They held to their traditions, laws, and rituals. Nothing could vary or change. Everything had to be done exactly right. There wasn't room in their "religion" for compassion or forgiveness. They avoided anything that was unclean (imperfect), including people. It's no wonder they had a problem with Jesus. Jesus associated with sinners. He saw past their imperfections and had compassion for them.

Jesus lived a perfect life. He taught us to love our neighbors as ourselves, to love our enemies, to pray for those who persecute us, to turn the other cheek, and to not judge others for their imperfections. Jesus then went on to willingly sacrifice himself for us. Romans 5:8 says that "while we were yet sinners, Christ died for us." He didn't require us to do anything in order to be good enough for him.

Many Christians live like the Pharisees. They have their lists of what they are allowed to do and what they aren't allowed to do. They do all they can to eliminate imperfections in their lives, including people. They have forgotten that the only way they are made perfect is through the shed blood of Christ. They have forgotten that the gospel requires us to reach out to everyone, regardless of their race, economic or social standing, political views, or culture.

We should seek to please the Lord with our lives. 1 Peter 1:16 tells us to "be holy, because I am holy." Holiness demands our obedience. It isn't easy and, in fact, sometimes it is rather messy. God doesn't judge our performance, but he looks at our heart. He is looking for a willing and contrite heart, one that is ready to learn from its mistakes and pursue truth and righteousness. We seek to please God, not those around us (1 Thessalonians 2:4). We find our worth and acceptance in God.

Abandoning the goal of perfection frees us from seeking approval from the world. The problem with perfectionism is that we try to achieve it ourselves. We try to live perfectly and all that brings to us is failure and defeat. It's easy to fall into the legalistic trap like the Pharisees did. Then we beat ourselves up because we don't measure up. We aren't ever good enough, and we don't deserve the grace God has given us. That's the point. We don't deserve it. That's why it is called grace and why Jesus had to die for us. If we could have done it all ourselves, Jesus' death would have been unnecessary. How tragic would that have been for the Son of God to give up his life for us, and we not even need him.

The good news is that the way to salvation isn't through living a perfect life. No matter what we do, we can never earn God's favor or his grace. Why? Because it isn't something we can earn. It is given freely to us as a gift. We must put down what Paul calls the "yoke of slavery" in Galatians 5:1 and start living by grace. Jesus said his "yoke is easy and his burden is light" (Matthew 11:30). Isn't that what we really want? The weight of perfectionism is a heavy burden to carry. Let Jesus take that from you and give you rest.

For further thought:

"If we claim to be without sin, we deceive ourselves and the truth is not in us." (1 John 1:8)

"For it is by grace you have been saved, through faith - and this is not from yourselves, it is the gift of God - not by works, so that no one can boast." (Ephesians 2:8-9)

"Are you so foolish? After beginning by means of the Spirit, are you now trying to finish by means of the flesh?" (Galatians 3:3)

24 THE STORM OF LOW SELF-ESTEEM

How do you decide how much something is worth? What gives it value? Is it what you use it for? Is it how many there are that are just like it? Is it where you can get one?

What gives you value? What are you worth? What would your parents say you are worth? Did they support you when you were growing up? Did they focus on what you did wrong? Did they ever tell you what you did right? Did they ever tell you anything that made you think you were of value to them? What about your children? What would they say you were worth? How about your spouse or your friends?

What do you think you are worth? What standard do you use to measure your worth? Do you compare yourself to others? Do you see everyone else as being better than you are? Do you see yourself as inadequate, inferior, and incompetent? Do you see yourself as worthless? Do you wish you were someone else?

How people see themselves will play out in how they live their lives. It is also connected to how they see God. People who struggle with self-esteem often see God as vindictive, stern, angry, controlling, and impersonal.[1] They don't think God can accept them because they can't accept themselves. They think they have to do something or be someone in order for others to love and accept them. They are always trying to figure out what they have to wear, own, read, listen to, talk about, think about, etc., in order to get others to like them. They spend their entire lives trying to live up to other people's expectations. They don't know who they are because they are constantly trying to be who they think someone else wants them to be.

Often times we get caught in the trap of putting ourselves down. We think things like: "I'm not pretty enough. I'm not smart enough. I'm not skinny enough. I'm not outgoing enough. I'm not a funny enough. I'm not successful enough." I've felt all of these things at some point in time in my life and what these thoughts do is tear down my self-esteem. Those kinds of thoughts deny that God is good and I am fearfully and wonderfully made (Psalm 139:14).

God knew what he was doing when he created each of us. To not accept ourselves is to say that God made a mistake when he created us. Are we forgetting that we are the clay, and he is the potter? (Isaiah 64:8) We had no say in how he created us or what plans he has for us. He knit us together in our mother's womb (Psalm 139:13). He didn't make a mistake in the way he distinctively formed each of us. We are created in his image (Genesis 1:27). We are image-bearers of God! There have been billions of people on this earth, and no two have been exactly the same. We are unique in our gifts, talents, and abilities. God loves us and created us exactly the way we are for a specific reason and purpose.

The Bible is full of examples of people who thought they weren't good enough. Moses is the first one that comes to my mind. God appeared to him in the burning bush and told him what his plans were. How did Moses respond? He told God that he was slow of speech and tongue. Moses was afraid that he couldn't talk well enough. How did God respond to Moses? Did he tell him he was wrong? Did he point out all the good qualities that Moses had so he would forget about this little speech issue? No. He came back to Moses with a question.

> The LORD said to him, "Who gave human beings their mouths? Who makes them deaf or mute? Who gives them sight or makes them blind? Is it not I, the LORD? Now go; I will help you speak and will teach you what to say." (Exodus 4:11-12)

The Lord promised to help Moses speak. He promised to teach him what to say. He told him not to worry about it, and that they would do it together. Isn't that what we all want to hear? Yet, even when the Lord promises these things, sometimes we still don't get it. Don't worry. We are in good company. Moses didn't get it either. He told the Lord to please get someone else. That response angered God. Why? Because Moses didn't trust God.

Below is a list of things to remember when trying to develop appropriate Christian self-esteem.

- We are chosen by God and, therefore, precious to God (Ephesians 1:4).
- We are not our own. We were bought with a price; the very blood of Jesus redeemed us (1 Corinthians 6:20).

- We are indwelt with the Holy Spirit. We are a new creature in Christ (2 Corinthians 5:17).
- We are justified by faith and accepted by God (Romans 3:28). We have been declared not guilty and not condemned (Romans 8:1). All charges of sin and wrong doing have been paid for.
- We have been adopted by God and are now a part of God's family. We are co-heirs with Christ (Romans 8:17).
- We are destined for glory (Romans 8:30).

As Christians, we should be always concentrating on the goodness of God, not on our own worth, not on our own ability. Our focus should be on the greatness of God. The problem is really not that we think too little of ourselves, but that we think too little of the God who created us. When we come to understand who God is and that he values us, then it doesn't matter what others think of us.

So to answer the original question, what gives you value? You are created and loved by God. He decides your value, and he valued you enough to send his Son to die for you (John 3:16). If he loves you that much, what right do you have to belittle yourself? Remember who you are in Christ, look at your unique set of gifts and talents, and enjoy being who God created you to be.

For further thought:

"The LORD does not look at the things people look at. People look at the outward appearance, but the LORD looks at the heart." (1 Samuel 16:7)

"When I consider your heavens, the work of your fingers, the moon and the stars, which you have set in place, what is mankind that you are mindful of them, human beings that you care for them? You have made them a little lower than the angels and crowned them with glory and honor." (Psalm 8:3-5)

"Yet you, Lord, are our Father. We are the clay, you are the potter; we are all the work of your hand." (Isaiah 64:8)

25 THE STORM OF JEALOUSY

Jealousy has been called the "green-eyed monster" and rightly so. It is an angry, strong, powerful emotion. It is destructive, selfish, and possessive. It is concerned first and foremost with me and my feelings. It wants to control others. It is cruel and unfair. It really boils down to selfishness and pride. It is one of the causes of broken homes and broken hearts. It refuses to tolerate a competitor. It is one of the most destructive forces in the world today.

Romans 12:15 tells us to weep with those who weep and rejoice with those who rejoice. Weeping with those who weep doesn't seem to be a problem. Most of us can empathize with another person's pain. Rejoicing with those who rejoice can sometimes be an issue. Especially if we are jealous of that person's success, family, or accomplishments. No one envies sorrow, but joy, that's a different story.

If we allow it to, jealousy can kill a friendship. How can we truly love our friends if we are jealous of them? It creeps into our lives in subtle ways. Pretty soon we hear ourselves saying things like: I wish I had the musical ability that he has. I wish I could teach the way he does. I wish I had a ministry like he has. I wish I had his gifts or his talents. As soon as we experience these kind of thoughts, get rid of them. What we are saying in essence is that we aren't satisfied with what God has given us or with how God has created us. Our problem is really dissatisfaction with God. What we need to do is stop comparing ourselves with others. We were each created as unique and special people. God had plans for us before we were even born. Think about those ideas. (Really meditate on the idea that God thinks we are special just the way we are.) What God has in mind for us to do and accomplish will be completely specific to our individual gifts and abilities. No one else can do the job that God created us to do as well as we can. We just need to seek God and figure out what that is. We must not feel bad for ourselves because we don't have someone else's gifts, talents, figure, money, etc. Our journey in life is completely unique.

What we don't see is that most of the people we are jealous of aren't satisfied with themselves. They are jealous of someone else. Often times what we are jealous of is something that other people had to really work hard at to accomplish. For example, if we are jealous of a musician, do we know how many hours he had to practice to get where he is? Are we willing to put that kind of work into it or do we just want the end result?

Sometimes we see kids who leave home for the first time and think they have to have everything their parents have. What they don't stop to consider is that their parents worked for years to afford what they have. They can't get it all instantly.

Let's think for a minute about the story of Joseph from Genesis 37. He was the 11th son of Jacob, and his half-brothers were jealous of him. Why? Because he was Jacob's favorite son. Jacob loved him because he was the son of his old age and the first child by his wife, Rachel. The Bible tells us that his brothers recognized that their father loved him the most and they hated Joseph. His brothers grew jealous of him. Joseph didn't help himself any when he started telling his brothers his dreams. When Joseph was seventeen, his brothers were off tending the flocks, and Jacob sent Joseph to check on them. His brothers took advantage of this situation. They threw him in a pit, and then sold him into slavery. They lied to their father and told him that a wild beast had killed Joseph. Joseph ended up in the house of the Pharaoh, and at his direction, was put in charge of storing up food for the upcoming famine. When the famine hit the land, Joseph's family came to Egypt to get food. The brothers came before Joseph, but they didn't recognize him. Joseph tested his brothers, and he learned how sorry they were for having treated him so badly. Joseph showed how God had healed his heart, and how he had grown in character when he forgave his brothers.

Thinking back through this story, sin led to more sin, which led to more sin, and pretty soon they were in so deep that they didn't know how to get out. The first sin was that his brothers were jealous. That moved to hatred, intense hatred, conspiracy, intent to murder, a refusal to listen to Joseph's cries for help (merciless treatment), selling their brother into slavery, deception, and lying. (I don't think this was the plan from the beginning; they just kept getting in deeper and deeper.) Think about the guilt with which they had to live. For 22 years they lived a lie. They never told their father the truth. They carried the guilt for the crime they committed. Even at the death of Jacob (Genesis 50:15-17), nearly 40 years later, they were still guilt-ridden. Joseph continued to reassure them that they were forgiven, and he reminded them of how God used a bad situation to save the family. But just think, this whole mess started over the "little" sin of jealousy.

Take a minute and examine your heart. Are you jealous of others? Are you envious of another person's job, family, house, lifestyle, or anything else? You are aware that this violates the tenth commandment. You know the one – the one about coveting (Exodus 20:17). Why do you think God included that one? He knew how destructive jealousy could be. The first murder was because Cain was jealous that God was more pleased with Abel's sacrifice than his own (Genesis 4). Jealousy is a dangerous emotion, and it needs to be recognized and dealt with.

Jealousy is hard to deal with because we don't want to admit it. It is easier to confess being angry than being jealous. It is an embarrassing fault to have. However, it is sin and like all other sin, it needs to be brought to the cross for forgiveness. Take a look at your life, and try to see why you were jealous to start with. Pray that God will allow you to not only be satisfied with what you have and who you are, but happy about all of it. Stop comparing yourself to others, and start loving yourself for who God made you to be. Pray that God will help you tame the green-eyed monster and give you the power to truly rejoice with those who rejoice.

For future thought:

"Anger is cruel and fury overwhelming, but who can stand before jealousy?" (Proverbs 27:4)

"Do nothing out of selfish ambition or vain conceit. Rather, in humility value others above yourselves." (Philippians 2:3)

"But if you harbor bitter envy and selfish ambition in your hearts, do not boast about it or deny the truth. Such 'wisdom' does not come down from heaven but is earthly, unspiritual, demonic. For where you have envy and selfish ambition, there you find disorder and every evil practice." (James 3:14-16)

26 THE STORM OF COMPROMISE

A big word in the world today is compromise. In some situations this is completely appropriate. For example, some people want red carpet in the church while others want blue. The groups come to a compromise and agree on brown. The men want to paint the bathrooms. The women want wallpaper. The groups compromise and paint the bathroom and add a wallpaper border. On issues like this, compromise is appropriate and effective. Each group gave a little on their position so that an overall agreement could be reached.

When you try to compromise on an absolute, there is a problem. For example, there is no room for compromise in the worlds of math and science. The law of gravity doesn't change. You can't ask it to overlook an object just this one time. Objects always fall down, they never fall up. Water always freezes at 32 degrees. Two plus two always equals four. A compass always points north. Why? Because that's how God set up the universe. If

God's laws were not absolute, always true, and always dependable, the universe would fall apart.

When we start compromising on what the Bible teaches, we run into spiritual problems. For example, the church as a whole, has compromised on our stance on divorce, abortion, same-sex marriage, immorality, and even godliness. We have become soft in our convictions and our character. We have become tolerant about unbelief. We bought into the world's view that says, "Why can't we all just get along?" In fact, I would say the world has gone so far as to say if we can't get along, then we'll just eliminate the Christian view from consideration. Christians have allowed this to penetrate our culture. We've compromised our faith and our convictions.

Daniel chapter 1 is a great example of a group of Christians standing by their principles and refusing to compromise. Jerusalem was invaded by Nebuchadnezzar. God allowed Jehoakim to be defeated. Then Nebuchadnezzar took the young men between the ages of 13 – 17 and his goal was to change their thinking. He was looking for "young men without any physical defect, handsome, showing aptitude for every kind of learning, well informed, quick to understand, and qualified to serve in the king's palace" (Daniel 1:4). He was going to teach them literature and the Chaldean language. He only wanted the best and the brightest for this project.

Daniel, Hananiah, Mishael and Azariah are selected. First consider why they were selected. They had worked hard. They looked good. They were educated. There's a principle here that we need to catch – God's people should be the best at whatever it is that they do. Not for man, not for money, not to get ahead, but simply because it pleases God. Because these men had performed with excellence, God was able to use them to accomplish great things. Some of us limit ourselves in ministry, because we don't give it our best, and that limits how God can use us.

Nebuchadnezzar's goal was to brainwash these men. He wanted to change the way they were used to thinking. They had been trained in the Jewish traditions. Now they were being taught the language and the literature of the Chaldeans.

This happens all the time in our world today. We raise our kids in Christian homes and then send them to public school. What do they learn there? Evolution is a scientific fact. Faith is irrelevant. America is not a Christian nation. Sex outside of marriage is OK as long as you're safe. The truth that we've tried to instill in our children is under attack. This is exactly what was going on with Daniel. Everything he had learned up to this point in his life was coming into question. Nebuchadnezzar even went so far as to assign the boys new names. He wanted everything from their heritage to be forgotten.

Daniel and his friends were then faced with the challenge of what to eat. They could very easily have just eaten what was provided. No one would have condemned them for that. After all, they were prisoners and would have just been doing what they were told in order to save their lives. Daniel 1:8 says, "But Daniel resolved not to defile himself." He made up his mind that he was not going to compromise God's law even if it meant his life. Daniel was a Jew and he was taught principles by his parents, and those guiding principles stayed with him even as he was in captivity in Babylon. So for Daniel, not eating the king's meat (which was probably pork) and not drinking the king's wine were not things on which he was willing to compromise. He was able to convince the guard to allow him and his friends to eat a simpler diet for ten days. At the end of ten days, the Bible says that they looked healthier than any of the others. God blessed them because they chose not to compromise their beliefs, but to trust him.

There have been many times in my life when I have been faced with these kinds of challenges. I haven't always made the right choice but I have learned a variety of lessons through compromising situations. Some of those include:

- God will provide what I need when I need it. He is always on time, although rarely early!
- I need to allow God to put me in the place where he has called me to be and be satisfied there, even if that place seems to be a lot like Babylon.
- I need to choose to be a woman of excellence and that takes time and commitment.
- I need to look to the Lord for wisdom and guidance and not trust in myself.
- I need to focus on doing my work for God's purposes and his glory; to bring praise and honor to his name.
- Compromise with the world will bring disastrous results. I reap what I sow. Sin always has consequences.
- No one is exempt from Satan's challenges, and he makes compromising in small things look innocent. Small compromises always lead to bigger challenges.

What about you? Are you ready to take a stand for what you know to be right? Have you determined in your mind not to compromise your faith no matter what obstacles you encounter?

For future thought:

"As obedient children, do not conform to the evil desires you had when you lived in ignorance. But just as he who called you is holy, so be holy in all you do; for it is written: 'Be holy, because I am holy.'" (1 Peter 1:14-16)

"Blessed are those whose ways are blameless, who walk according to the law of the LORD.

Blessed are those who keep his statutes and seek him with all their heart — they do no wrong but follow his ways. You have laid down precepts that are to be fully obeyed." (Psalm 119:1-4)

27 THE STORM OF CHOICES

We are all faced with choices every day, and the choices we make will shape our lives not only now, but into the future. Think about some of those major choices that we have had to make. Things like what school to attend, what church to join, whom to marry, what job to take, where to live, etc. All of these things have shaped not only our lives, but the lives of people around us. Therefore it is crucial that we make good, biblical choices.

Sometimes we know what we are supposed to do, but it is still hard to make that decision. We are prone to choose the easy way out. Jesus talked about this idea in Matthew 7:13 -14:

> Enter through the narrow gate. For wide is the gate and broad is the road that leads to destruction, and many enter through it. But small is the gate and narrow the road that leads to life, and only a few find it.

The narrow way is often much more difficult right now, but is always the right choice. For example, the narrow way may mean letting go of a relationship that was leading us in the wrong direction, and that is hard because we really like that person.

Many times we make the wrong choice because Satan makes that wrong choice look so good. He never shows us the full price that we will have to pay for that choice up front though. We need to pray for wisdom and discernment. We need to be willing to call evil, evil, and good, good. We need to be careful not to compromise on little things, because small compromises lead to bigger and bigger ones. We don't sin in a vacuum; our choices affect others around us. For example, consider when David sinned with Bathsheba (2 Samuel 11). Who had to pay for that sin? The obvious answer is David, but think about it a little farther. Bathsheba had to pay. Uriah had to pay – it cost him his life. David's son had to pay. That innocent child's life was taken because of David's sin.

Let's look at another example. What about when the Israelites were about to enter the Promised Land, and they sent in 12 spies? The job of the spies was to report back about the crops and the lay of the land. Joshua and Caleb came out with a good report. They believed that God would help them take the land. The other 10 spies saw the fortified cities and the giants, and were so overcome by fear that they encouraged the people not to enter. Their sin, of not trusting God, cost the nation of Israel 40 years of wandering in the desert (Numbers 13). An entire generation of people died in the wilderness as a result of this sin.

So we make a bad choice, then what. Galatians 6:7 says that we reap what we sow. Or in other words, our choices bring consequences. If we make a bad choice, we need to own up to it. Admit our mistake – both to God, and to anyone else affected, ask for forgiveness, make restitution if necessary, learn from our mistake, and then move on. This process is called repentance. Repentance is necessary if we are going to have any kind of a relationship with God.

I've made some bad choices in my life. It's not fun to deal with them, but it is necessary. I have learned that people respect a person who is honest and can own up to his/her mistakes. Saying you are sorry and asking for forgiveness goes a long way in mending a relationship. I've also experienced people who couldn't do this simple process. They just couldn't admit when they were at fault. I find people like this to be really hard to deal with and difficult to trust. But their problem is really one of pride, and that is something God will deal with them about. 2 Corinthians 5:10 says that we will all appear before the judgment seat of Christ and have to give an account for what we've done. God will have the final say in all matters.

How do you keep from making bad choices? You need to pray and ask God for wisdom (James 1:5). You need to study the Word of God. Sometimes the Bible will speak directly to your situation. If God has spoken clearly about the situation, just obey. If you are still in doubt, seek the advice of godly council. Find someone whom you know will give you solid Biblical council, and talk to him. This might be your pastor, but it might also be a friend whom you know has a good relationship with God, and knows the Word. The key here is to make sure it is godly council, and then listen to him. It doesn't help you if you get advice, and then ignore it. What good is that! Think through the decision and try to see the impact it will make, not only on yourself, but on the people around you.

How will this decision affect you spiritually? For example, you are thinking of taking a new job. The new job will provide more income and improve your status, but it will cost you time with your family, and will interfere with your ability to attend church. If it detracts from your relationship with God, don't do it. Is this decision going to line up with what God has created you to do? God created you with specific gifts and talents (1 Peter 4:10). Will this allow you to use those? Will it allow you to do it for his glory? Sometimes things look good on the outside, but when you seek God about it, there's no peace in your heart. Make no mistake; God will give you an inner peace as a guide. Use caution if making a decision that goes against that inner peace (Philippians 4:7).

In Joshua 24:15, Joshua tells the people of Israel that they need to choose who they are going to serve. The Israelites were quick to bail out on God when things got tough. They often made poor choices and lived like the pagan people around them. They wanted to be like everyone else. Things aren't so different today. The world is constantly trying to make us fit into its mold. We need to make a choice, choose the lifestyle of the world, or choose to serve the Lord. Our choices will determine our destiny. If we choose not to serve the Lord, we have chosen the broad road that leads to destruction. It may be easier for the moment, but in the long run, it will bring pain and heartache.

Jesus made the tough choice. He chose the narrow path. He made the decision to go to the cross and die. It was his choice to make. No one else could make it for him. I'm glad he made that decision. Just like David's choice affected others around him, Jesus' choice has affected people for eternity. We now have the option of also choosing the narrow path, that path that follows in the steps of our Savior. We get to choose to serve him, live for him, and eventually be with him forever.

We each must make our own choice. Which path is it going to be for you, broad or narrow?

For further thought:

"Trust in the LORD with all your heart and lean not on your own understanding." (Proverbs 3:5)

"There is a way that appears to be right, but in the end it leads to death." (Proverbs 14:12)

"The way of fools seems right to them, but the wise listen to advice." (Proverbs 12:15)

"But if serving the LORD seems undesirable to you, then choose for yourselves this day whom you will serve, whether the gods your ancestors served beyond the Euphrates, or the gods of the Amorites, in whose land you are living. But as for me and my household, we will serve the LORD." (Joshua 24:15)

28 THE STORM OF IDOLATRY

We are all looking for something to worship. One of the constant themes in the Bible is one of idolatry. The Israelites really struggled with it. One of the reasons God commanded them not to intermarry with other cultures is because he knew that they would compromise their faith. In fact, the history of Israel is really a story of idol worship, punishment, restoration and forgiveness, only to repeat the whole pattern again and again. The prophets continued to warn the people, who continued to ignore them until it was too late, and God's wrath was poured out on them. Then they repented and the process started over again. We are so blessed that our God is a long-suffering and merciful God, because over and over again, he forgave them and restored them.

Idolatry is not just an Old Testament issue. It wasn't just the Jews who struggled with it, everyone struggles with idols. An idol is anything that we give a higher priority in our lives than God. It could be something tangible like our spouse, children, jobs, homes, cell phones, big screen TVs, or cars. It may be something like our love for sports or shopping. It could even be our computers or what we spend time doing on our computers. It could take the form of alcohol, drugs, sex, or any other sin. It might not be sinful in itself; it just becomes sin when it becomes our priority. For example, even the work we do for our church can become an idol, if it becomes more important in our lives than our relationship with Christ.

We look to our idols to provide us with what only God can give us – our sense of self-worth. We think we can do things on our own, without God. We forget the first commandment – "You shall have no other gods before me" (Exodus 20:3). We get ourselves into trouble because we are depending on ourselves. The root of idolatry really comes back to a heart attitude of pride, self-centeredness, greed, and a love for material things. All of these are a form of rebellion against God. God can't stand it, and he will do whatever he needs to do to get us to see the idols in our lives.

Sometimes we don't intend to let things take that priority in our lives. They just seem to creep in there. God has had to teach me this lesson over and over again. When I was in college, I worshipped at the altar of softball. It was the most important thing in my life. God allowed me to make the college team only for me to discover that it no longer brought me joy. When I was in my 40s, I became quite successful in my career. I started to become proud of my achievements. I was doing really well and was well respected in my field. Then God got hold of my heart and made me see that I was actually putting my job ahead of him in my life. Time and time again, just like the Israelites, God has had to show me this in my life. Each time as I repented, he was gracious to forgive and restore our relationship.

I have a friend whose idol was her marriage. Her security was wrapped up in her husband. It gave her a sense of belonging. Then she went through a really rough time in her marriage and started questioning her own self-worth. Her marital problems made her feel hopeless and overwhelmed. She felt rejected by her husband and abandoned by God. Yet God was there all the time, waiting for her to repent and choose to give him first place in her life. She needed to remember that her self-worth was in who she was in Christ, regardless of what was going on in her marriage. None of that means that she didn't still love her husband. But until Christ was first, she couldn't forgive her husband and love him the way God was calling her to love him.

You could say that all other sin has its roots in idolatry. Idolatry is deceptive and sneaky. Idols can creep into your life when you least expect them. For most people, it is subtle enough that it is hard to notice and, therefore, even harder to deal with. The real question is, is God the most important thing in your life? Do you love the Lord with all your heart, soul, and mind, as Jesus commanded us to do in Matthew 22:37? No one can make this decision for you. God can't even make this decision for you. Only you can decide. Will you give God first place in your life?

For further thought:

"Do not store up for yourselves treasures on earth, where moths and vermin destroy, and where thieves break in and steal. But store up for yourselves treasures in heaven, where moths and vermin do not destroy, and where thieves do not break in and steal. For where your treasure is, there your heart will be also." (Matthew 6:19-21)

"No one can serve two masters. Either you will hate the one and love the other, or you will be devoted to the one and despise the other. You cannot serve both God and money." (Matthew 6:24)

"Therefore, I urge you, brothers and sisters, in view of God's mercy, to offer your bodies as a living sacrifice, holy and pleasing to God - this is your true and proper worship." (Romans 12:1)

29 THE STORM OF REGRET

We all have regrets from our past. There are things we wish we hadn't done, or things we didn't do, that we wish we had. How many times have you wished you could go back in time and change something? Regret haunts us all. It keeps us from experiencing God's joy and power in our lives.

Take Adam and Eve for example. They lived in a perfect garden. Everything around them was good. They had perfect minds and bodies. They walked with God and experienced his presence. They were also created with free will, and the given the opportunity to make choices. They made a bad choice and once it was done, it couldn't be undone. By choosing to listen to Satan and disobey God, sin entered the world. Not only were they affected, but all of creation was affected. Disease and death entered the world for the first time (Genesis 3). Thankfully, God had a plan to redeem the world through Jesus. But how do you think Adam and Eve felt after their choice, after their sin? I am sure they lived the rest of their lives in regret. They mourned their mistake. While forgiveness was there, they couldn't undo what they had done.

Regret can also be a good thing when it motivates us to action. Paul is a good example of this. Prior his salvation, Paul persecuted Christians. He hunted them down and sought to destroy the church. He was vigilant and determined. Galatians 1:13 says, "For you have heard of my previous way of life in Judaism, how intensely I persecuted the church of God and tried to destroy it."

Then he met Jesus on the road to Damascus, and he experienced the love and forgiveness of Christ. Even though he was forgiven, he knew what he had done. Paul writes to Timothy, "Even though I was once a blasphemer and a persecutor and a violent man, I was shown mercy because I acted in ignorance and unbelief" (1 Timothy 1:13). He did not consider himself worthy of the grace that he was shown. In 1 Corinthians 15:9 he says, "For I am the least of the apostles and do not even deserve to be called an apostle, because I persecuted the church of God." However, he didn't say these things in order to obtain pity from others. He used his past to motivate him in serving the Lord. He allowed his past to fuel his zeal for the Lord.

I have many things in my life that I regret. I regret some decisions I made – some of them quite major. I regret lost opportunities. One place I worked, I had opportunities to lead Bible studies and go on mission trips. I kept thinking I'll do that next year. Then pretty soon there weren't any more next years. I regret not spending more time with my daughter when she was growing up, but I needed to work. This list could go on for pages. There are many things in my life that I would change, but we don't get to go back and do it again.

So what do we do with regret? The book of Psalms is a place that I frequently go to when I need encouragement. The writers often cry out to God and ask for help. They don't cover up their feelings or act like they have it all together, but they cry to God for help with the issues in their lives. I'm so thankful that they were transparent enough to allow us to see their hearts and to permit us to see a correct way to handle the problems that life throws at us. The Psalms show us a God who hears, answers, loves, and forgives. They show us that God is righteous, but also that God cares about every detail of our lives, that God shows mercy even when we don't deserve it, and that God is patient with us even through all our mistakes and struggles.

Do you remember the movie, "Bucket List"? It came out in 2008 and starred Morgan Freeman and Jack Nicholson. The main idea of the movie was that these two men were terminally ill, and they made a list of things they wanted to do before they died. They wanted to do things like go sky diving, ride motorcycles on the Great Wall of China, and fly over the North Pole. And so one by one, they checked things off their list only to find that these things really didn't matter that much to them. In the end they discovered that their friendship was what really mattered.

Wherever we are in our lives, we should make a spiritual bucket list. What things do we want to do for God while we can? God wants us to live our lives in complete submission to him. As we do that and seek his will for our lives, we can live our lives with no regrets. I have never once regretted doing anything that the Lord led me to do.

While I have all kinds of regrets, I don't think God has any regrets for my past. He does not look at my past and wish it could be changed. He looks at my past to see how he can redeem it. He wants to use it all to show me his love and grace. He looks at what I can't change, and uses it to change me, help me grow in my faith, and to continue to conform me to the image of Christ. That's his ultimate goal for me (Romans 8:29). The key to the whole thing is that I have to let him do it. I have to allow God to redeem my mistakes. I have to give him control over all my life. I continue to hold on to things and live in regret, because I don't want to give up control. I keep searching for the power to fix what is broken, when the reality is that I can't fix anything on my own. I need to surrender it all to God – my past, present, and future. It's time to stop relying on myself and start trusting God to work all things together for good (Romans 8:28). It takes faith to let go.

Whatever you've done in your past, God can redeem it. You can rest knowing that even though you can't change your past, God can change your future. Commit everything to God, trust him, and never look back.

For further thought:

"For I am convinced that neither death nor life, neither angels nor demons, neither the present nor the future, nor any powers, neither height nor depth, nor anything else in all creation, will be able to separate us from the love of God that is in Christ Jesus our Lord." (Romans 8:38-39)

"Brothers and sisters, I do not consider myself yet to have taken hold of it. But one thing I do: Forgetting what is behind and straining toward what is ahead, I press on toward the goal to win the prize for which God has called me heavenward in Christ Jesus." (Philippians 3:13-14)

30 WHERE DO I GO FROM HERE?

Everyone has difficult times in life. It isn't a matter of *if* trouble will come. It is *when* trouble comes, how will I survive? When I am getting clobbered by the world, how will I deal with it? God doesn't shield us from difficult times. However, he will help us get through it. He will make us "more than conquerors" (Romans 8:37).

I have often wondered why God would let us encounter some of the difficulties we have experienced in our lives. I think sometimes he allows things to happen in our lives to teach us lessons that can only be learned in the midst of strife and turmoil. Sometimes the difficulties we are going through are our own fault. They are consequences to sin. Sometimes the difficulties are just the result of living in a fallen world. When Adam sinned and sin entered the world, so did some of the difficulties of life. We need to trust God and persevere through them.

God believes in us sometimes more than we believe in ourselves. He knows we will get through it, and be better for it in the long run. Some things can only be learned through first-hand experience. Like young boys learning to play baseball, we have to get in the game to really see what we can do. It's only when life knocks us down that we really know we have the strength to get back up and do it again.

When we find ourselves stumbling in our relationship with God, disappointed in a decision we've made, frustrated with words we spoken, or upset with how we reacted in a crisis, we shouldn't stay down long. We have a God who loves us, forgives us, and wants us to get back up and persevere through it.

"We are hard pressed on every side, but not crushed; perplexed, but not in despair; persecuted, but not abandoned; struck down, but not destroyed" (2 Corinthians 4:8-9).

We aren't defined by our failures, but by what we do with them. We will have our ups and downs, our good days and our bad, our triumphs and our defeats. That is part of life. Remember that we are never alone. Jesus is always there.

Let's look at one final story from the Bible. In Matthew 8 we find the story of Jesus calming the storm. He had been teaching near the Sea of Galilee, and he needed quiet time. He and a couple of the disciples got on a boat and headed toward the opposite shore. It wasn't too long until Jesus was asleep and a storm arose. Most likely, the disciples onboard were familiar with storms at sea, but this storm was unlike what they had experienced before. It was so fierce that they were afraid they would die. The waves were breaking into the boat and the boat was filling with water. Where was Jesus? - sound asleep. When they woke Jesus, he rebuked them for their lack of faith. Aren't we just like the disciples? We get so overwhelmed by the storms in our life: betrayal, discontentment, doubt, mourning, etc., that we forget to just go and rest with Jesus. He's not going to let the boat sink while he's aboard. When God allows a storm in our lives, it comes with a purpose. If we miss the purpose, we miss the blessing, too.

Let go of your fear, grab hold of your faith, and let the storms come. Faith in Christ is all you need, because he alone can calm the storms and get you to the other side. There is Hope in the Midst of the Storm!

AFTERWARD

This book has been addressed to Christians and discusses how God can help you get through anything life can throw at you. If you aren't a Christian, if you've never repented of your sin and asked Jesus to forgive you, that is where you need to start.

Romans 3:23 says, "All have sinned and fallen short of the glory of God."

Romans 6:23 explains that the penalty for sin is death - separation from God in hell forever. No matter how hard you or I try, we cannot save ourselves. We can't earn our way to heaven with our good works, with our church attendance, or with our baptism.

Jesus came and lived a perfect, sinless life. He willingly died on the cross to pay the penalty for our sins. Three days later, he rose from the dead proving his power and authority. Jesus provides for us a way to have a relationship with God the Father, and he provides eternal life for us through his death and resurrection.

Romans 10:9 says, "If you confess with your mouth Jesus as Lord, and believe in your heart that God raised him from the dead, you will be saved." If you have never entered into a relationship with God, please know that the God who created you, loves you no matter what you've done. He longs for you to experience his forgiveness and his grace.

All you have to do is reach out to him and tell him that you are willing to trust him for salvation. You can use your own words or the simple prayer below:

> Jesus, I know I am a sinner. Please forgive me of my sin and save me from eternal separation from God. By faith, I accept your work and death on the cross as a payment for my sin. Thank you for loving me and forgiving me. Thank you for making me a child of God today. Please give me the strength and wisdom I need to follow you and obey you. In Jesus' name, Amen.

If you've made the decision to accept Jesus as your Savior, it is important that you find a local church where you can begin to grow in your faith and learn more about God through his Word.

NOTES

Chapter 2:Worry

    1. Corrie Ten Boom. BrainyQuote.com. Xplore Inc, 2014. 28 October 2014.
http://www.brainyquote.com/quotes/quotes/c/corrietenb135203.html

Chapter 3: Brokenness

    1. Charles Stanley, *The Blessings of Brokenness* (Grand Rapids: Zondervan, 1997),
28-29.

    2. Ibid., 69-70.

Chapter 6: Doubt

    1. Johnnie Moore, *Honestly [Really Living What We Say We Believe]* (Eugene:
Harvest House Publishers, 2011), 35-38.

    2. Ibid.

Chapter 7:Fear

    1. Vicki Tiede, *Healing Your Wounded Heart*(Greensboro:New Growth Press,
2012), 64.

Chapter 13: Apathy

    1. Francis Chan, *Crazy Love* (Colorado Springs:David C. Cook, 2008), 68-79.

Chapter 15: Stress

    1. http://dictionary.reference.com/browse/stress?s=t. November 3, 2014.

Chapter 20: Lies/Deceit

    1. http://dictionary.reference.com/browse/lying. November 3, 2014.

    2. Eric Hetvile, "Less Than Three Percent Of Those Who Say They'll Pray For You
Actually Ever Do" http://www.freewoodpost.com/2013/02/18/less-than-three-
percent-of-those-who-say-theyll-pray-for-you-actually-ever-do. October 31,
2014.

Chapter 24: Low Self-Esteem

    1. P Cox, "*Self-Esteem*", Message by Paul Cox, Crystal Lake, IL 1984.

ABOUT THE AUTHOR

CAROL HORNER taught in Christian schools in the Atlanta, Georgia, area for 25 years. In 2012 she and her husband, Randy, returned to Bedford County, Pennsylvania, to be near their families. Carol is currently the technology director at the Grier School in Tyrone, PA.

She earned a B.S. from Lock Haven University, an M.Ed. from Covenant College, and an Ed.S. from Liberty University. An active member of Chestnut Ridge Independent Fellowship Church in Fishertown, PA, Carol currently teaches an adult Sunday school class, sings in the choir, serves on the worship team, and co-leads a women's Bible study.

Made in the USA
Charleston, SC
21 January 2015